FRANCIS BACON

Michel Leiris

FRANCIS BACON

RIZZOLI
NEW YORK

© 1987 Ediciones Polígrafa, S. A.

Translated by John Weightman

Reproduction rights: Francis Bacon
Photograph credit, page 2: Hans Namuth

First published in the United States
of America in 1988 by:

RIZZOLI INTERNATIONAL PUBLICATIONS, INC.
597 Fifth Avenue/New York 10017

Library of Congress Cataloging-in-Publication Data

Leiris, Michel, 1901-
    Francis Bacon.

    Translation of: Francis Bacon, face et profil.
    Bibliography: p.
    1. Bacon, Francis, 1909-   —Psychology.
2. Portrait painting, English—Psychological aspects.
3. Portrait painting—20th century—England—Psychological
aspects.   I. Title.
ND1329.B27L4413   1988   759.2   87-28552
ISBN 0-8478-0904-8

Printed in Spain by La Polígrafa, S. A.
Parets del Vallès (Barcelona)
Dep. Leg.: B. 38.594 - 1987

Francis Bacon, full face and in profile

Orestes, only just released from persecution by the Eumenides; Hamlet reassembling his wits after the encounter with the Ghost; Don Juan, no more of a superman than his cowardly valet, but straining every nerve to defy the hell to which the Commander has doomed him; Maldoror, half-angel half-ogre, recovering his breath after the prolonged blasphemy of *Les Chants*; a sort of Falstaff, now jovial now reflective, whose debaucheries have left him looking almost as youthful as when he was a page in the Duke of Norfolk's household; a lucky gambler, directly aware of every aspect of our contemporary upheavals, and whose elegantly modern silhouette we seem to glimpse at that precise moment, wholly outside clock-time, when he stakes his all on a throw of the dice, a hand of cards or the roulette wheel...

Francis Bacon's clean-shaven face, at once chubby and tormented, and as roseate as that of some eighteenth-century English empirical philosopher discoursing over his brandy or his sherry, seems to reflect wide-eyed astonishment as well as an intelligent stubbornness and — allied to a hidden fury — the sensitive distress of a man who has not forgotten that he was once a child whom almost anything could move to wonder. His forelock, which is well in evidence in all his self-portraits, like a reckless comma staunchly inscribed across his brow, appears to be there as an emblem showing that, inside his head, nothing proceeds according to the lazy norms of some already accepted pattern, but that everything is liable to be called into question, cut short or left in suspense. Perhaps it is this same rejection of ready-made solutions which is indicated by his slightly askew — or, at any rate, not at all full-frontal — stance in many of his photographs; like his walk, always, one might think, on the point of breaking into a dance, it could signify a distaste for the sedate tranquillity of those who have never felt the ground crumbling away beneath their feet.

In contrast to the casual but always irreproachable clothes worn by Bacon, the man (a character irreducible to any single expression) — who, incidentally, should also be seen, with no romantic aura, as the glutton for work he really is, up early every morning, however he may have spent the night before —, the untidiness of his studio, a cluttered mews flat with a permanently littered floor, set in the well-groomed calm of a London residential area, seems, by its very shambles, to call obviously and imperatively for that relative creation of order symbolically represented by the painting of a picture, and, at the same time, to provide for its owner, who has allowed so much lumber (painting materials, scattered photographs damaged by neglect, etc.) to accumulate in the place where he habitually sleeps and no less habitually paints, a three-dimensional equivalent of Leonardo da Vinci's famous, and richly suggestive, wall.

Is it not the case that art, whether it gives an account of things as they exist or depends essentially on the play of the imagination, has, as its ultimate function, to save us from disaster by creating, alongside the everyday world, another realm, fashioned according to the requirements of the human spirit and in keeping with an inner order which, by its very nature, is in sharp contrast to the unbelievable muddle of the reality around us? And is there not something comparable between settled, civilized sites, which hold the encircling wilderness at bay thanks to an ordered lay-out of one kind or another, and the plastic arts as creators of images on which the human gaze can fasten, images which, being entities different in essence from the myriad constituents of the external world, provide us, as it were, with points of anchorage? This being so, the artist, once we admit that his activity goes beyond mere entertainment, could be said to find his *raison d'être* in the very existence of the chaos in which we flounder, since, in this confusion, his role is to make his own statement, his own personal statement, tenuous though it may be (and in a truly human voice of a kind that our expressly utilitarian creations cannot echo). Although difficult to describe in respect of his appearance, which is hard to classify within any strict framework, Bacon may, as a painter who insists on being nothing but a painter and less the practitioner of an art than of a ludic activity conveying no message, have an individual tone of voice less resistant to definition.

As if the picture had its own life, and constituted a new reality instead of being a mere simulacrum, an oblique allusion or some appropriately symmetrical pattern (with no more bite to it than a piece of pure ornamentation), that feature in a Bacon canvas which is immediately apprehended and asserts itself unequivocally and independently of any sense of agreement or disagreement — whatever the elements brought into play, and even when the theme of the work puts it on the level of myth rather than of everyday reality — is the kind of *real presence* to which his figures attain, even though this presence has no connection at all with any kind of theology. Through the agency of the figures, the spectator who approaches them with no preconceived ideas, gains direct access to an order of flesh-and-blood reality not unlike the paroxysmal experience provided in everyday life by the physical act of love. And this presence is graced with a wild ambiguity, an alluring iridescence, which makes it a sensuous delight, but one so intense that, despite the attractiveness of its painterly vehicle, to some people, repelled perhaps by its searing impact, it can appear wholly abhorrent.

Far from producing a mere surface excitement or picturesque effect, Bacon's works continue to disturb, to charge — even retrospectively — with good and evil, the always to some extent surprising moment of their initial apprehension, and this is a virtue which bears manifest witness to their exceptional quality. What, after all, is the point of a painting devoid of this ability to obsess, and which, after we have communed with it for some time, seems to be little more than an accident breaking the monotony of the wall against which it hangs? The only works which truly exist and achieve full reality are those which establish a persistent hold over us — as, indeed, can also be the case, since it is quality not duration which matters, with such ephemeral things as a song, an actor's performance or a dance — and influence our subsequent ways of thinking and feeling, instead of simply providing us with an impression, striking and moving no doubt at the time, but which, since it has produced no change in our emotional apprehension of the world, did not carry us beyond the limits of dilettantism.

What Bacon offers in most of his paintings, to whichever phase in his development they may belong, are — leaving aside their purely accessory or decorative elements — depictions of living people or normally banal objects — endowed, or at least apparently so, with a certain figurative veracity directly referential to phenomena experienced through the medium of the senses or, more generally, the sensibility, but about which one can obviously say that, far from being reflections of the surrounding world like those of photography, they result from a completely free use of the technical resources of painting and are likenesses whose nature as painted fictions tends, however, to pass unnoticed, so that they exist more forcefully than any simple representation (they are, it seems to me, entities of a particular type, and not simulacra devoid of independent life). In other words, it could be argued that Bacon's essential aim is not so much to produce a picture that will be an object worth looking at, as to use the canvas as a theatre of operations for the assertion of certain realities. In this respect — although, while making no vain effort to be modern, he undoubtedly belongs to the second half of the twentieth century both through his style and the elements he brings into play — he differs not only from the Surrealists (who, being obsessed with dreams and inventions of a phantasmatical kind, turned their painting into a receptive screen for highly imaginary projections) but also from the Cubists (for whom the validity of painting, as a radical transposition of a motif that was either real or supposed to be so, lay in its strongly structured composition, free of any optical trickery), and again from their great predecessors, the Impressionists (for whom a picture was an open window or a key-hole, flattering the eye with some luminous or filtered fragment of the everyday world).

Avoiding any use of dramatic lighting (since it would incline his work towards a form of Expressionism, whereas he categorically repudiates this tendency and, as a realist contemptuous of bombastic effects and theatrical or satirical intentions, seeks to translate his sensations in as literal and as persuasive a manner as possible), or of delicate or brilliant visual ingenuities (in the style of the Impressionists), Bacon usually stands the object to be painted in harsh, steady electric light or, occasionally, in clear sunlight unmitigated by anything reminiscent of the weather, so that all is exposed, as it were, to a midday glare — midday being a temporal peak and *the moment of truth* — or in the equivalent of what, in theatrical parlance, is called ''lights full up''. Can we not, then, conclude from this that, throughout his work, this multifaceted artist insists on putting all his cards on the table and — being equally averse both to shilly-shallying and old-fashioned niceties — pays cash down, as it were, in that ''immediacy'', which he agrees is characteristic of some of his works, as he explains to the art historian, David Sylvester, in one of their dialogues transcribed from long tape-recordings — there are four dialogues in the 1975 edition, seven in the revised edition of 1980 and an eighth, as yet unpublished — which could be continued indefinitely, given the insistence shown by the two speakers in trying to dispel any ambiguity in relation to the questions discussed — exemplary documents, showing how far removed Bacon is from wishing to maintain any coy reticence about his work and how his apparent untidiness goes hand in hand with a rare intellectual rectitude? An immediacy due, I should say, not only to the suddenness of the effect produced but also to the abrupt challenge with which the spectator finds himself unceremoniously faced, on a par (it would seem) with the artist himself, who is always deeply implicated in his work, just as he can be seen to be directly involved in his unambiguous replies to the implacable questioning of his shrewd and persistent inquisitor.

The space in which we breathe and the time in which we live here and now: this is what we find, almost without exception, in Bacon's pictures, which seem to aim at the immediate expression of something immediate, and which cannot be adequately described simply by saying that, in general, they avoid the exotic and the archaic, the only works not respecting this rule being *Landscape with a Rhinoceros* (1952, based on a photograph taken in Equatorial Africa, and in any case one of the canvases later destroyed by the artist, as has happened with many others), *Man Carrying a Child* (1956, a memory of a long stay in Tangier), the *Popes* (1949-1952), inspired by the famous painting of Innocent X by Velázquez, and the portraits of Van Gogh (1957), — some of them slightly Fauvist in treatment — which are anachronistic up to a point, being almost, but not quite, of the present. Between most of Bacon's pictures — in this connection, at least, I would like to emphasize his singularity — and the people looking at them, the proximity is indeed greater than if their themes merely involved no spatial or temporal distancing. Although such pictures have no relationship with *trompe l'œil* (an ersatz by which, in any case, no-one is seriously deceived), and the artist has ensured that they are authentic creations, equally distinct from both abstract and what he pejoratively terms ''illustrational'' or ''illustrative'' art, it could be said about them that they make the spectator feel as if he *were there*, or even *is actually there* (inside the picture, not simply in front of it), a form of words which expresses the feeling of total participation and, in this sense, goes further than Roland Barthes' trenchant phrase, *that is*, which he applies to photography in his undeniably illuminating book, *Camera Lucida*, to indicate that the past is replaced by the present: *that was* signifying that the paradoxical function of photography is not so much to offer an immediate and artless representation of phenomena as retrospectively to bear witness, since the process is by definition retrospective, and to assert authoritatively that something has existed or occurred.

In many of Bacon's canvases, those which — according to my admittedly subjective point of view — seem the most typical, in other words, those belonging to the period of full maturity, by which time this self-taught artist had, without benefit of any formal instruction and, as it were, through sheer physical effort, provided himself with a technique, objects are shown to us in a space delineated (approximately) according to the traditional rules of perspective, and are correspondingly convincing. They are quite close to us, apparently life-size, and they seem to rest on a floor which might be an extension of that on which we are standing as we look at the picture. It is as if we were no longer pure spectators, but were actually involved with the objects. In such pictures — which certainly have their own kind of geometry but, as it were, of a peripheral sort (relating only to the marginal areas), and not affecting the figures, which are too freely handled to be reducible to simple structures — the overall construction seems to correspond less to a decorative, or strictly plastic, intention than to the requirements of the total organization, presentation or operativeness of the elements, — both on the part of the artist building up the work and that of the spectator, whose eyes and mind are caught and expressly compelled into participation. Being usually closed and exiguous, the space of the picture — an area which appears to be neither a substitute for our world nor a small-scale model of it, but its actual reflection — seems to constitute — whether it happens to be a featureless room or some outdoor, and invariably banal, space — a kind of box in which, ideally, the spectator himself is included, and thus fictitiously introduced into the very place where the object, apparently on the same scale as himself, is on show for him, and where, having been promoted from the innocent role of a mere armchair observer to that of a *voyeur* fully present at the quasi-anecdotal, but non-summarizable, episode set before him, and trapped in a space more often than not enclosed in itself but still open to him, he can be imaginatively present — to which end, indeed, the whole artistic apparatus seems to have been organized.

The space, then, in which we live, but our time as well. Many of Bacon's works, in addition to containing elements drawn from his personal history (he was a furniture designer for a while, before his vocation as a painter declared itself, more or less, one might say, as painterly qualities declare themselves within the frigid structures of the canvases), are apparently conceived with the intention of making their topicality obvious. Contemporaneousness is a feature of the dress worn by the human figures and of the (invariably functional) furniture they make use of, as well as of the other accessories, all strictly relevant to the present time: electric light-bulbs or switches, rugs, umbrellas, safety-razors, wash-basins and lavatory seats, telephones, cameras, illegible newspapers (their tattered fragments, littering the floor, convey an impression of untidiness analogous to the real untidiness in the artist's studio), half-smoked cigarettes (again as if to emphasize, by reference to a precise moment, the picture's quality of being taken from real life or caught *in flagrante delicto*, like a Joycean epiphany), arrows which seem to be borrowed from traffic-signs or from drawings relating to movement, such as are to be found in technical handbooks, and so on. All this material is dealt with not so much pictorially as in a strictly informative style (with no aestheticization of the industrial object, such as is usual in Fernand Léger's work or, to a greater or lesser extent, in Man Ray's ''rayographs''). Just as, by other means, the space of the picture is rendered in terms of our space as spectators, so Bacon seems to be determined clearly to signify that what he is seeking to invest with an appearance of life is situated — as everything authentically alive must by definition be — in a time which can be none other than our own. The clothes (always modern and commonplace) or the nakedness (totally non-classical) of Bacon's characters, might be his or ours at this very moment.

Bacon's painting, while doubly immediate (its effect is immediate and it deals almost always with the here and now), has the further characteristic of conveying no message, as he categorically states in one of his first dialogues with David Sylvester, at the same time as he rightly objects to being too hastily labelled an Expressionist. Is it not obvious that his aim is to practise a form of painting devoid of, as it were, any form of distancing? Art of this kind, just as it excludes remoteness in space or time, cannot tolerate that other sort of non-immediacy which might be called reflective distancing: that which characterizes art requiring an effort of thought for its full, and always to some extent postponed, appreciation, since it proceeds by allusions calling for more or less lengthy interpretation, and its action, far from operating with instantaneous effect, only makes itself felt with some delay, after a roundabout process which obviously diminishes its impact, while perhaps increasing its resonance.

Although, both in its texture and in its iconography, Bacon's painting is not at all austere, it can be said to exemplify a paring down, in the sense that it shows a complete disregard for symbols, or for anything that might suggest associations with folklore or with extraordinary phenomena foreign to our everyday context. A paring down which, in its essence, is comparable to that of games or gambling, as might be expected in the case of someone who is not only a real-life gambler (devoted to roulette, that rapid, and wholly aleatory game of chance), but who also believes that painting, having completely lost its sacralizing function in the modern world, can now be no more than a game (a very debatable view, one must admit, since it disregards the fact that painting can still have an educational role, however misapplied). Can we not say that, like art as Bacon conceives of it (a demystified art, cleansed both of its religious halo and its moral dimension — two aspects which were almost one and the same — and hence profoundly realistic, even in those rarer cases where the habitué of the bar of the late Muriel Belcher, of whom he painted several portraits, makes no attempt to render any external reality but endeavours to make real, to give irrefutable body to, something purely internal and perceptible only to himself), games or gambling — activities with no inherent justification but to which one can nevertheless devote oneself with deadly consequences — are essentially things of the immediate moment, valid in the present (not according to any finality involving subsequent effects), and devoid of any meaning outside their sheer practice?

If, as he maintains, art, in the contemporary world, can be nothing more than a game (a very different concept from that of *art for art's sake*, since it implies no special valorization tending to replace sanctifying art by the sanctification of art itself), how far can it be said that Bacon, with his perfectly secular mind closed to any possibility of transcendence, goes beyond pure entertainment in practising this game, to which he appears to be still more passionately attached than he is to classic games of chance?

Unlike Picasso, that other practitioner of a very great game who seemed to delight in trying out the most diverse methods of coveying meaning and so called into question the whole language of painting, Bacon — very similar in this respect to his contemporary, Alberto Giacometti — appears to have striven to be a figurative artist of the most accurate and effective kind possible. In his case, the game consists not so much in the invention of signs as in the struggle between the artist and what he aims at signifying, a contest which, being the interplay between the contingent nature of the theme and the image the artist makes of it by trusting to his subjective impulses, engenders the ''tension'' that Bacon is looking for and which, in his opinion, is inevitably lacking in non-figurative works.

Apart from a few large canvases of an undeniably tragic nature, which for the most part take the nowadays unusual form of triptychs, and a small number of works whose themes are borrowed from natural phenomena other than man (animals, one or two landscapes, grass, a jet of water, a sand dune), Bacon's favourite subject is, manifestly, the living reality of human beings. In this connection, it is notable that his work although quite varied, includes no example of a still-life — if we except *Study for a Figure* (1945-1946), which consists simply of a folded overcoat next to a hat and a pile of flowers, and the half-open travel-bag in the central panel of the 1967 triptych, inspired by, but revealing no visible connection with, T.S. Eliot's "Aristophanic melodrama", *Sweeney Agonistes* — and also notable that even water and sand, when he makes use of them, appear to be inhabited by some violent gushing or swirling movement which gives them a semblance of life, the life that Bacon, whether he is transcribing or inventing, seems to be trying above all to express, instead of attempting to remould and then reconstitute the form or contours of the subject, whether real or imaginary, and thus perhaps endow them with a meaning. In fact, I would go so far as to say that Bacon's most Bacon-like pictures are those which, in their general structure as well as in the treatment of the figures, suggest the rhythm of life. Just as, in the real world, the exceptional moments (in which adventure occurs) stand out against the humdrum nature of ordinary living, so the backgrounds of these pictures — like calm waters — are broken here and there by patches of virulent painting which, in contrast to the coolness of the surrounding *décor*, seem to be like fissures through which the painter's sacred fire, non-domesticated at these points, is burning in total freedom. As one observes him exploiting this opposition between a clearly established order and the disorder within it, one is confirmed in the view that — through artistic intuition more than by any logical process — he must have gradually discovered the necessity of a difference in potential if the current is to flow and to give rise to something resembling life.

In a Bacon canvas, then, there are incandescent parts, seething with energy, in contrast to neutral parts where nothing is happening. The former, which defy rational control and are comparable to what in jazz are called "breaks", solos grafted onto the beat of the basic rhythm — i.e., in more classical terms, frenzied or Dionysiac parts contrasting with calm, Apollonian parts — might be thought of, if we bring in a romantic reference to Stéphane Mallarmé, that poet of flame and crystal who used the black-and-white pattern of a typographical lay-out not unlike newspaper headlines to give a lofty metaphysical dimension to a game of absolute chance, as areas where the dice are thrown hurricane-like (where the great game is being played), the other areas being little more than *the undifferentiated neutrality of the abyss*, serving only to constitute the place where certain entities manifest their pictorial presence as if to contradict the formula defining the inane: *nothing will take place but the place*. That place, in this instance, is practically non-existent yet must be perceived as a place (painting being essentially a matter of direct sensory perception). Therefore it demands to be clearly established as a place, although in fact it has little claim to appear, serving as it does merely to house the character, or characters, who give life to the picture, as if it were a sort of abstract annexe of the real place where the work is on exhibition and the spectator is standing, and were there to provide a continuity allowing the latter to gain a foothold in the area containing the opaque density of the figures, which are so close to him, appear contemporaneous with him, and with which he cannot help but identify to some extent.

Given the fact that, on the one hand, the invention of photography relieved painting of any "reporting" function (as Bacon points out), so that it is free to develop its own modes of figuration, while, on the other hand, it is impossible for a painter simply to copy the figure he is dealing with to give an impression of reality because, if he does so, the deception is immediately obvious, recourse must now be had to something other than photographic transcription. The spectator will have a chance of believing in the figure presented only if it bears the living mark of the artist's hand (failing this, no contact will be established), and only if there is some degree of distancing, even though this distancing may be violent enough to give rise to a mis-understanding, so that the profoundly realistic tenor of works such as those of Bacon and his glorious predecessor, Picasso, is explained in terms of Expressionist intentions, whereas, in fact, they contain no caricatural exaggeration relating to what Bacon refers to pejoratively as "illustrational" art, but correspond to a more radical and more difficult ambition, which is to operate a plastic remodelling in depth. Using distortions not motivated by a dramatic, or even a purely aesthetic, intention, Bacon, in painting a figure, seeks to translate a true or fictitious reality about whose immediate and actual existence the spectator will entertain no doubt, once he sees it projected almost life-size onto the canvas as a representation cleansed of all those habitual ways of looking at things which, in the ordinary process of living, prevent us, or almost prevent us, from seeing it — a displaced representation breaking the visual routine which obliterates perception, and yet reminding us of the times and of the setting in wich we live; and the artist's practice, in doing so, is something akin to transmutation and, like transmutation, subject to numerous chance effects. Consequently, in more than one instance, there is so severe a distortion of the forms that some admirer of Oscar Wilde might be led to conclude too hastily that, reversing the operation of Dorian Gray's magic portrait, which protected the real-life appearance of the hero by taking his gradual decay entirely upon itself, Bacon's portraits, as if endowed with some prescient power, show their models from the outset as creatures already attacked by decay.

Contrary to what one might be inclined to think, presence — an enigmatic quality, independent of aesthetic systems and resistant to analysis — is not a matter of style: it may be missing from a highly elaborated painting demanding an effort of interpre-tation and a considerable measure of participation from us, the interchangeable spectators (as if presence, which constitutes the very life of the picture, were nothing other than the presence of the figure composing itself in our minds as spectators, on the basis of the immediate data of perception), but, conversely, it may charac-terize some almost naturalistic work, whose subject-matter offers no difficulty of appre-hension.

In the case of Bacon's pictures — at least those I consider to be most curiously alive, irrespective of any question of quality — their extreme intensity seems to me to result from the paradoxical conjunction of two procedures: a more or less marked distortion of the figures, combined with a fairly naturalistic treatment of their surroundings. Being a surprise factor (in view of its remoteness from what one might reasonably have expected), such a marriage of hot and cold cannot fail to arouse attention and heighten the sensation of presence. But this unlikely union is only one example amongst others of the contradictions characteristic both of Bacon's life and of his artistic practice: in a given picture, the coexistence — which I again emphasize — of large areas treated with apparent indifference (backgrounds in flat tints) and of sections produced by what one might call *pictura picturans*, a form of painting which seems to result from a sudden unleashing of mental, as well as manual, energy (the figures); a relatively geometrical patterning of the setting, the firm arrangement of which stands in opposition to the sometimes almost indefinable form of the figures which, in some cases, seem to lose their bone structure to become strange fluxes or whorls of matter in fusion; and, in the portraits essentially, the liberties arising from the decision not to be illustrational and the constraints imposed by the determination to arrive at an exact resemblance, in so far as it is possible for the painter to square the circle by rendering his subjective and quasi-arbitrary reaction to what he knows of the character's external appearance without disregarding the public data supplied by photography which, in this instance, is used not as a source of inspiration but as a "control" (in the form of photographs of the passport kind, as far removed as possible from the "artistic" variety and devoid of anything that might influence the imagination, and serving therefore as mere guide-lines, not as catalysts, as was the case, for instance, with some of Muybridge's work dating from the end of the nineteenth century and dealing with bodily postures and movements, or medical photographs of the insides of mouths such as have often provided Bacon with a documentary starting-point for his work); the wholly secular nature of an art which insists on being nothing more than a game and, with realistic intent, attributes no other role to its themes than to be what they are, whereas, on the formal level, leaving aside the direct references to religious paintings (such as the *Crucifixions* which, for the most part, have no iconographical relationship with the death of Christ but are elaborated in triptych form, as if for the purpose of some edifying ceremonial that has lost its content but kept the pattern of its ritual, just as for James Joyce, Bacon's near-compatriot and near-contemporary, the pattern of the ancient *Odyssey* served as a model for that of his very modern *Ulysses*), — whereas, I say, Bacon's art, at once suitably composed and furiously spontaneous, not only makes great use of a convergence between modernity and tradition (hence its frequent recourse to the eminently classical form of the triptych which, as it were, enfolds the spectator within itself and — so Bacon has told me — was suggested to him by the panoramic screens of certain cinemas) but also, since its cool framework so often seems intended to restrain an almost savage violence, appears to be marked by a surface ritualism at least, just as, on a quite different plane, that of everyday life, the discipline of English good breeding — decorum in private relationships — is, with Bacon, a discipline of pure courtesy, and by no means excludes unruliness or tends to act as a censor of desire.

The distortion is so acute that it borders on disruption and, to say the least, suggests that André Breton's assertion: *beauty will be convulsive or not exist at all* has been raised to the status of a principle demanding absolute obedience, — an alteration of natural forms which may be carried to the point of blurring or even obliteration, — in one way or another a profound upheaval, the disturbing, disconcerting and, for some people, scandalous character of which arises from the fact that when Bacon seeks to convey the feeling of (not to describe) some given or invented reality, and for this purpose resorts to distortion, he does not simply alter the form (in the manner of the Cubists who, in calling so magnificently into question all the traditional means of the language of painting, tended to disregard the materiality of objects in order to concentrate on their outlines) but also the substance of the motif, and in particular the flesh of the model, which is rendered in its very warmth and elasticity, both of these features being indicative of life. Bacon's abrupt departure from a literal representation of the motif with the sole aim of rediscovering it in a more telling form undoubtedly constitutes a more thorough and more real onslaught on the real than if he limited his assault to the structure: the distortion is apprehended all the more strongly as such in that the motif is in no way robbed of its materiality, and moreover is rendered as being expressly immediate (therefore in close proximity to us), and is, in general, accompanied by a comparatively naturalistic respect for perspective in the treatment of the setting and even in the overall definition of the figure.

Not only are Bacon's characters devoid of any psychological dimension, always presented in their substantiality and, when appropriate, clad in some form of dress — set before us, then, in their strictly physical, as well as social, existence — the painter shows himself to be as literally materialistic in his work as might be expected of someone who, in discussing his conception of painting, refers to his "nervous system" rather than his personality, thus demonstrating his refusal to idealize even in his choice of words, and who, besides, makes no use in his work of drawing as such, as if he wished to avoid its abstract unreality and preferred the direct application of paint with the brush or some other means, so as to put himself, as it were, in direct contact with the object: not only remodelling the forms but kneading the very matter itself in the shape of coloured pastes and other ingredients, perhaps the most suitable procedure for someone like Bacon, who wants to reach the deepest level, the substratum, and who, by treating appearances with the greatest freedom, is not so much trying to express the real thing, whether perceived or conceived but in either case interpreted in a largely subjective mode, as seeking to render — if I may so put it — the reality of the thing, its very existence, apprehended (if this were possible) over and above its circumstantial features, so as to keep no more than its biting essence, an essence that Bacon, by paradoxical means, appears to convey with extreme sharpness, through some fluke almost comparable to the isolation of that ''cutting'' virtue, supposedly held in reserve in as yet unblunted razor-blades, at least according to a literal acceptance of Marcel Duchamp's ''pataphysical'' humour.

To strip down the thing so as to retain only its naked reality — such, no doubt, is Bacon's aim, although the thing in question may be only one element among others of the general image of the work in progress (the basis of the effort to embody the particular image that has occurred to him, although, during the pursuance of the effort, more often than not a quite different image will replace the original one), and although it may, in most cases, be something realistic in spirit but imaginary, and not a motif borrowed from the external world, such borrowing being by now very rare in Bacon's case, since he paints his portraits from memory, with the help of photographs and without asking his subjects to pose, the actual presence of the sitter inhibiting him, he says, when he is submitting the image to the desired distortions (and perhaps, generally speaking, because, for him, contact with the living reality to be painted is something so poignant that he cannot contemplate it except through the intermediary agency of photography). These distortions are necessary audacities since, but for them, the image would be no more than an effigy, whereas Bacon, thirsting for irrefutable presence, appears unable to restrict himself to evoking representations of real or imaginary people or things so as simply to fill the surface of the canvas, but to insist, however arbitrarily they may be treated, on giving them positive existence in the fictitious space allotted to them. Since, in his case, sensation, either direct or mediated through photography, takes precedence over ideation, and since his chief driving-force is a vehement desire to grasp reality, we can say that Bacon has a frenzied, as well as an effusive, approach to that reality which, above all others, he is endeavouring to translate, and that this frantic, almost panic, urge produces an emotional breaching of boundaries which introduces, into the texture of the canvas, the disturbance felt by the artist himself, so that it is less through deliberate than through what might be called affective, distancing (often carried so far that the artist appears to be creating figures on the point of overflowing or in a state of liquefaction) that he achieves the sensation of presence, unobtainable otherwise either by a copy or an intellectual transcription.

''*Tentative de capturer l'apparence avec l'ensemble des sensations que cette apparence particulière suscite en moi*'' (An attempt to capture the appearance together with the cluster of sensations that the appearance arouses in me): such was Bacon's definition of realism in a letter to me, written in French with the help of a common friend, although in fact he has an excellent command of the language but is always afraid that his knowledge will be inadequate for the precise and totally unambiguous expression of his thought in the kind of rigorous discussion he seems to enjoy. ''It may be that realism, in its most profound expression, is always subjective'', was another remark in the same letter, following up various conversations we had previously had on the subject, a general concern of mine at the time, and during one of which he had pointed out that there are ''inner realities'', and that realism in art must not be confused with the simple desire to give a translation, in convincing terms, of objectively existing phenomena.

The motif, whether discovered or imagined — obtained from without or within, selected in broad daylight or wrested from darkness — after being treated by the artist in his role as presenter or fabricator, must give the consumer the feeling of being confronted with a new reality, weightier than an image; such, in my view, is the meaning of realism as understood by Bacon, a realism — comparable to that of Picasso, amongst others — which is not simply transcriptive but creative, is less concerned to represent than to establish reality, and may even, thematically, go beyond the limits of verisimilitude, without however acquiring any tincture of idealisation. It is an extreme kind of art, beautifully exemplified in the overpowering 1982 picture, originally the central panel of a triptych that was later reduced to a single canvas, which shows a male body, a solid mass of flesh, resting on a table the four legs of which are all on the same line, a body reduced to an armless, headless trunk with blatant sexual attributes and crowned with two hillocks in the form of a pulpy, skywards-facing rump, a compact idol which also includes — besides a pair of heavily shod feet — two legs half hidden by cricket-pads, impedimenta which seem to immobilize them like splints and thus, through a kind of antiphrasis, to make them more keenly perceptible as living limbs. It was followed, also during 1982, by its female equivalent (a headless trunk crowned by two breasts, inspired by an Ingres drawing), and by another male torso (richly sculptured but without stiffness, since it is presented in movement, and is not the only as it were "Futurist" attempt by Bacon to follow a body in its action).

Not being "slices of life" in the manner of the works of the Naturalist school of writers, Bacon's most strictly realistic, but non-anecdotal, pictures are more in the nature of flash photographs comparable to Joycean epiphanies, banalities coinciding so perfectly with their formulation that they are suddenly raised to the level of disturbing presences, as, for instance; the *Dog* coming towards us more or less blindly (1952) or accompanied by its master's shadow (*Man with Dog*, 1953); a young man, whose speed cleaves the air we breathe as, with windswept hair, he rushes forward on his bicycle (*Portrait of George Dyer Riding a Bicycle*, 1966); a woman standing on a pavement, where we also seem to be, while a car goes by on the roadway beyond (*Portrait of Isabel Rawsthorne Standing in a Street in Soho*, 1967); two replicas of Leopold Bloom, in felt hats, sitting side by side as if for the exchange of probably trivial remarks, but that we feel we might overhear if we so wished (*Two Seated Figures*, 1979).

Although the theme of a Bacon painting is never anecdotal, or at least the power of the painted surface, invariably unenhanced by any eye-catching title, never depends on the actual or supposed event referred to — a homosexual coupling, for instance, or, in a 1971 triptych, a man preparing to ascend a dimly lit staircase, and recognizable as the George Dyer of many other paintings, who had died tragically not long before — we can say that a canvas of this kind is, first and foremost, a space in which something occurs, takes place, or comes into being in a sort of "happening" which, in the last analysis, is none other than the revelation of the presence aimed at in all Bacon's works, and without which the overtly manual activity from which it results would remain null and void. More often than not, it is a human presence, but it may also be, so to speak, the elemental presence of a fragment of nature devoid of anything that might resemble a soul: the grassy space forming the motif of the 1978 *Landscape* (reduced, more or less, to a duly circumscribed sample of grass, so that the transcription is given more force through compression), the 1979 jet of water (achieved through an actual projection of liquid), the 1981 sand dune (the result of rubbing or pulverization), and more recently — as the artist himself has told me — water from a running tap. When this presence is the human presence, which seems, throughout his different phases, to remain Bacon's major objective — always falling short of the absoluteness he aims at — he may make use of various devices, quite remote from Expressionism, to produce an oblique intensification, as, for instance, in several canvases or triptychs painted in the sixties and seventies: a shadow taking the eminently material form of a pool or blot that seems to have been secreted by the figure, which thereby acquires greater weight; a reflection, like an appendage or a double with the same density as the original, so that the latter's reality is confirmed by the repetition; the omission of part of the body under consideration or, conversely, its emphasizing through some addition (the Verist painting-in of splints or other accessories intended to offset a physical handicap but which, in fact, highlight it more than they conceal it) or, sometimes also, the problematic or even acrobatic positioning of the body in an apparently unbalanced attitude or on the point of falling, and so, one might say, more conscious of itself and therefore more telling in its effect on the spectator; sometimes, even, a bodily movement which is all the more striking through not being accomplished in the normal way (for instance, a man using his foot to turn a door-key, the main theme of *Painting*, 1978). The search, often by the most roundabout means, for an immediately perceptible reality — or, more precisely, for a concrete resonance thanks to which the onlooker has the feeling of entering into immediate communication with the real — such seems to be Bacon's artistic endeavour, which is always conducted in a state of extreme tension, since it is through the active interplay of contrary forces — the urge towards realism and the desire to transcribe in total freedom — in other words, by more than a romantic, and purely external, juxtaposition of contrasts, that the artist has the best chance of achieving his aim: to secure the supreme manifestation of a presence in all its ''brutality of fact'' (the expression used by Bacon himself in his discussions with David Sylvester), and to subjugate the spectator by the peculiar life his gaze kindles in this presence.

But, for the two-dimensional figures inscribed on the canvas to be invested with such compelling life, although we know it to be artificial (independent of biology and a product of human ingeniousness), is it enough that the figure should appear not as a passive copy of a certain reality, but as an inventive, imaginative recreation of that reality, and should speak to us about something quite close to us in space and time? Whether or not Bacon has been aware of any inadequacy in this respect, the fact is that — no doubt spontaneously, and less through calculated effect than in the heat of the moment — he has never had the slightest hesitation in introducing irrational elements into the painting and organization of his pictures, and this influx of illogicality has given them a still greater charge of life. Not only has he always relied a great deal on what, in his conversations with David Sylvester, he calls ''accident'' (a drip of paint from the brush, whether fine or broad, a slip of the hand, or any other involuntary mishap modifying the intended effect) and has even gambled on a deliberate recourse to chance (by throwing paint directly at the canvas or rubbing it over with a rag, thus producing aleatory effects which have at least the advantage of reducing the ''illustrational'' nature of the given painting, and even of allowing work to go forward on a different basis), he has also often slipped in apparently gratuitous details without any thematic justification or, even if they can be accounted for by some artistic requirement, that requirement was sufficiently vague for the painter to satisfy it in a resolutely arbitrary fashion, so that the canvas, thus divorced from all ideal norms, patently bears the stamp of that contingency inherent in all manifestations of life on this planet. Such vagaries — closed or open circles, ellipses or indefinitely shaped blots, distributed, as far as one can tell, at random; pointing arrows, which not only catch the eye, but seem to be intended to deflect the gaze in a certain direction; or again, a long trail of white paint suggesting a sudden outflow or a whiplash — act as heightening accents in the sense that, having no meaning or being pure signals, they exist to some extent as capricious or disorderly elements (expressive of liberties taken or rules broken) in relation to the comparative order of the meaningful whole which, but for the touch of madness thus introduced, would be a more or less interesting or attractive or even fascinating composition, but not the thing, vibrant with life, that, in its essential uncertainty, it is.

Galvanize the figure or figures, punctuate the proffered spectacle according to whim, instead of obeying imperatives of composition (which would be to tend towards decoration) — such, in my view, is one of the golden rules applied instinctively, or so one imagines, by Bacon. This may explain why, for instance, he has sometimes taken a given figure and, by recasting or even twisting rather than by literally reconstructing it, squeezed it, wholly or partially, into a more restricted framework, supplementary to the general framework of the picture: this addition may be a totally nonrepresentational, purely linear pattern which, at the same time as it serves as an intermediary term between the figure and the actual picture-frame, and up to a point helps to suggest the space in which the figure is supposed to be, seems to constitute a cage, visible only in bare outline, and into which the figure has been more or less packed, as though, in order to ensure maximum force, the freely and furiously painted part had to be enclosed, set like a jewel, or enshrined, just as, with the same purpose of intensification, Bacon sometimes puts it against a screen, another simple means of enhancement.

Whether he gives them definite location thanks to a semblance of geometrical patterning, or whether he supplies a background which serves to set them off, it seems that Bacon often arranges for certain parts of a picture to be isolated for emphasis, or to stand out as being the dominant parts: those which, because of their theme, are the most lively, and in relation to which the other parts are no more than a background, a place laid out for the action. It is with the same intention, no doubt, that he likes to lift his figures up, either by means of a modest pedestal supporting the piece of furniture on which the particular figure is seated or lying, or by frankly raising them from the floor (as in the 1970 triptych, which presents three female figures perched on a sort of long curved beam running acrosss the three panels, or in another triptych of the same year in which the two lateral panels are occupied by a man sitting on a seat apparently attached to supports, like the seat of a swing). It is worth noting, incidentally, that Bacon, in discussing his art, reveals — as a simple fact, without trying to analyse its causes, which can be presumed to operate at some deep and decisive level — his particular interest in elevated figures, at least, be it added, when they are human. He mentions, for instance, that he was very impressed — from the secular point of view of the pure spectacle — by a photograph of Pope Pius XII borne aloft in the *sedia gestatoria* on the occasion of his enthronement, and he admits that what interests him in the theme of the Crucifixion is not the religious drama, with the divine victim as its central character, but — apart from the act of butchery ojectively characterized by the event — the spatial position of the hanging Christ elevated on the cross. No doubt, Bacon's art, materialized in paintings far removed from any form of belief and, as he himself says, conveying no message, is much too secular and positivistic for the term ''sacred'' to be applied to it with any confidence. Nevertheless, it is the case that this same art, which he claims is no more than a game, and which brings him substantial rewards, a fact which he does not pretend to disregard but, on the contrary, humorously enphasizes (a debunking approach, resulting to some extent from Dadaist nihilism and from the calling into question not only of traditional aesthetic systems but of the very value of art itself, and therefore of the ''artistic'' attitude), does frequently give rise to works which can legitimately be regarded as having a sacred aura, not of course as a result of their content since — the point must again be stressed — they are profoundly realistic pictures, devoid of any transcendental allusion, so that what they offer is offered with no hint of anything beyond the given representation, but because each particular work seems to be ruled by conventions singling out certain elements which are made to appear all the more imbued with life through having been visibly separated off from the profane banality of the humdrum (saved from the commonplace, wrenched out of ordinariness, placed either literally or figuratively on a podium, by means of various devices underlying what painting has achieved in those areas where painterly frenzy has, as if by a happy chance, been unleashed). The isolation, by various methods, of the figures as if, in spite of their prosaic nature, they were untouchable idols; their ambiguity, since, without being Expressionist, they are often distorted to the point of inspiring a feeling akin to that blend of ecstasy and anguish which is known as sacred horror, and which is perhaps experienced most acutely in those vertiginous moments, prompted by the most widely different causes, when we have the sensation of entering into intimate contact with ultimately revealed reality; in the case of several of the figures, a partial blurring which seems to give them a deliberately secret character, without in any way detracting from their realism; the solemnity of the overall arrangement, especially in the triptychs, but innocent of any aspiration to the sublime, and all the more effective because of this; the frequent intervention, as in the paintings of previous centuries with their pious representations of donors, of assessors or sometimes of assessors once removed (assessors of assessors, as it were) who, like officiating priests or acolytes, seem to have their appointed place in some hierarchical ceremonial and to act as a guard of honour for the main figure, who is thereby invested with still greater prestige, just as, in other contexts, Bacon may achieve a heightening effect by painting pictures within the picture, such as male heads which are obviously portrait busts... Is it not legitimate to suppose that all these features are intended to confer one precise quality on the works in which they occur: the power to entangle the spectator in the toils of what might be called a *blank* liturgy which, having no transcendental references whatsoever, and existing only for its own sake, is all the more moving through being quite untinged by any dubious implications?

Being a realist, since, even when he allows himself to go beyond the bounds of verisimilitude, his ultimate aim seems to be to express life (the life we live and feel, the being in flux that each one of us is) and to produce work endowed with that presence which is its own peculiar life, directly perceived without any intervening haze of mental distance, — an authentic realist but an enemy of the anecdotal which, even when serious, never penetrates below the surface foam of reality — Bacon has taken care not to burden his canvases with anything strictly speaking dramatic, that is, not to bring into play any story-line, which, being accessible to the intellect, might short-circuit, and thus weaken, the sensory impact of the work, and at most has made use of almost non-existent scenarios (the most pronounced, no doubt, is in the central panel of the 1965 *Crucifixion*, where a man, scarcely visible except for his tricolour cockade, is being molested by some-one wearing a swastika armband, a detail which, according to the artist, has no historical significance and was motivated simply by the need to put a patch of colour in that particular spot and by the circumstance that the arm-band was suggested by an old coloured magazine photograph showing Hitler surrounded by other Nazis). The fact remains, however, that, being too devoted to life to reject even the mortal counterpart implied by its lack of fixity, he has on several occasions accepted the idea, not assuredly of drama — too close to everyday newspaper stories and too involved with narrative — but of tragedy which, while avoiding sentimental overtones, appeals to that part of his sensitivity affected by ''the smell of death'' he finds in places where butcher-meat is on display. Not only do the various *Crucifixions*, from which the Bible story was immediately and totally excluded, remain marked with a seal of blood (mangled flesh), but also a very early triptych (*Three Studies for Figures at the Base of a Crucifixion*, 1944) is based on one of the darkest themes of Greek mythology, the revenge of the Eumenides, and another more recent one (1981) was expressly inspired by the *Oresteia* of Aeschylus. However, it is obvious that even though this composition has a tragic quality, it is undoubtedly free of all pathos and devoid of the slightest theatrical element: the qualities operative in this direct and simple work are the firmness of the general structure and the marmoreal solidity of the figures presented, qualities in keeping with the true nature of tragedy which, unlike drama where the characters behave according to their feelings and the play of circumstance, makes its protagonists beings all of a piece, subject to harsh necessity or fatality. Here again, without any recourse to the anecdotal, Bacon displays his profoundly realistic approach even in the use of myth: what he puts on show for us is quite simply there, like an epiphany, and of too dense a texture for us to deny it. Such is also the case with the 1976 triptych, which preceded the one just mentioned, and has as its central theme a man — a Promethean figure, one might say — whose head is being pierced and ripped apart by a bird of prey with outstretched wings, a bird akin to the more modest one to be seen standing below the flayed carcass of an animal (apparently a pig) in the 1980 picture entitled *Carcase of Meat and Bird of Prey*, another work that it would be impossible to translate into a story or any sort of developed statement, but which achieves the tragic resonance of a sacrificial scene through the majestic quality of its structure and of the colour of the piece of hanging butcher's meat. Finally, it should be noted that, in painting the *Bullfights* of 1969 whose truthfulness is all the more astonishing in that they are not the work of an aficionado, Bacon dealt realistically with what many of us consider to be one of the surviving manifestations of ancient tragedy.

Behind their glass which, according to him, is a means of "unifying" material unevennesses in the painting, but which I suspect is also intended to temper to some extent the realistic virulence of the works, or perhaps to give a certain ceremonial dignity to the presentation of characters caught, it would seem, more often than not in the warm tangle of erotic exchange, or in the most commonplace waking or sleeping attitudes, not to mention the most grossly functional ones, or again to extend to the whole picture (including the flat background) and to finalize, thanks to an almost literal englobing, that process of setting apart, of removal from the neutrality of everyday life, which is achieved, as regards certain of its features, by the most diverse means, Bacon's canvases, at once so effervescent and so controlled, provide, for the spectator who looks at them as a whole and grasps them in their diversity, a striking image of this unique contemporary artist in all his complexity, a complexity I had hoped markedly to reduce by studying him in the mirror of his work. The hope was, more or less, vain: to portray Bacon's art, even with the help of his instructive discussions with his friend, David Sylvester, turns out in the end to be almost as difficult as to draw the portrait of the artist himself, and hardly more enlightening (more conducive to simplification). Failure would, then, be undeniable if, after this rapid survey which makes no claim to detect hidden symbolic meanings where none is meant to be looked for, it were not after all possible to suggest, in a very general way, the significance of Bacon's work.

Although the artist himself declares that he has no message to deliver, I have found from personal experience that his pictures help us, most powerfully, to feel the sheer fact of existence as it is sensed by a man without illusions. In this particular instance, the sensation is all the more acute in that painting — in a present time clearly established with a wealth of detail — appears abruptly as a presence, both for its own sake and as a source of images which, in works that are operative and immediate in the effect they make on us and in their temporal topicality, have as their only purpose to be an almost wounding presence. Moreover, is it not a fact that such art, almost every image of which represents a sovereign conjunction of beauty and its negation, echoes the dual nature of those moments that we appreciate as being the most specifically human ones, those in which — fascinated, entranced to the point of vertigo — we feel we are in touch with reality itself and are at last living our life, while at the same time realizing that our delight is flawed with a strange dissonance: the anguish aroused by that hostile immanence, death, which any apparently total grasp of life reveals as being lodged in our most intimate being? It is perhaps this fundamental ambiguity, above all, which prompts Bacon, a hyper-sensitive artist with a fierce thirst for reality, to treat the reality he creates in his paintings as others might treat a sacred entity: using various devices, he puts it in inverted commas or singles it out for emphasis, as something marvellous, the ambiguous nature of which (half-magic, half-menace) incites us to stifle it as much as to laud it.

In relation to these canvases, whose deep-rooted modernity is not reducible to a mere surface piquancy, David Sylvester uses the word "relevance", thus crediting them with the quality of being exactly apposite, of doing and saying what needs to be done and said. These pictures, having no hidden depths and calling for no inter-pretation other than the apprehension of what is immediately visible, since the artist forestalls all ideological commentary by denying any intention of implying more than he paints, and being spaces filled with pure living presences indicative of nothing other than themselves, and therefore stamped with an absence of sense — with, in other words, *nonsense* — seem, in their dazzling nakedness of the very moment (a nakedness with neither hither side nor beyond and unencumbered by anything in the least literary), to be images in keeping with the inanity of our situation in the world as ephemeral beings, more capable than other living creatures of brilliant and pointless ecstasies. In short, they correspond to that modern state of mind, referred to in a previous generation as *le mal du siècle* — the ardent awareness of being a presence permeable to all the charms of a world not notable, however, for its kindness, and the icy certainty that we are no more than this, have no real power, and are what we are only for a ridiculously limited time.

Like Samuel Beckett, whose apparently non-mysterious sentences are reminiscent of the discreet emanations from a smouldering peat fire, Francis Bacon — without rhetorical inflation or mythological paraphrase and in ways capable of providing total enjoyment through the accuracy and vigour of the formulation, whereas by rights we should be overcome by the harsh truthfulness of what is being thus tacitly suggested — expresses the human condition as it truly and peculiarly is today (man dispossessed of any durable paradise when able to contemplate himself clear-sightedly), and consequently he can with justification be called a realist, however strong — on a less everyday level — the tragic element that comes through unmis-takably in places, but is also explicitly expressed both in the *Oresteia* triptych and in the allusions to the Eumenides (direct in the *Three Studies for Figures at the Base of a Crucifixion*, and indirect in the free plastic paraphrase of *Sweeney Agonistes*, a poem in one epigraph of which, derived from the *Choephori*, Orestes speaks about his persecutors). While the most solid achievement of an artist of this kind, operating with a directly figurative intention, is to make the fascinated spectator immediately aware of the bizarre, indeed absurd, nature of his existence (as a contingent, but questioning, being with no transcendent dimension), at the same time he cannot do other — even without aiming at pathos — than show the appalling dark side of life, which is the reverse of its bright surface. As an authentic expression of Western man in our time, Francis Bacon's work conveys, in the admirably Nietzschean formula he himself has coined to explain the sort of man and artist he is, an "exhilarated despair", and so — however resolutely it may avoid anything in the nature of sermon-izing — it cannot but reflect the painful yet lyrical disturbance felt by all those who, living in these times of horror spangled with enchantment, can contemplate them with lucidity.

CHRONOLOGY

1909. Born in Dublin, 28 October, of English parents, the second of five children. Father a breeder and trainer of racehorses. He is a collateral descendant of the famous Elizabethan philosopher, Francis Bacon.

1914. At the outbreak of war, the family moves to London and his father joins the War Office. Thereafter they move back and forth between England and Ireland, changing houses every year or two — never having a permanent home.

1925. Bacon suffers from asthma as a child and is privately tutored — never has any schooling in the conventional sense. Leaves home at the age of 16 to go to London. Works for a short time as a servant to a solicitor and later in an office for several months.

1927-28. Travels to Berlin, stays for two months only, then on to Paris where he occasionally secures commissions for interior decoration. Visits a Picasso exhibition at the Paul Rosenberg Gallery which greatly impresses him and inspires him to start making drawings and watercolours.

1929. Returns to London. Exhibits in his Queensbury Mews studio furniture and rugs made from his own designs. Begins painting in oils (self-taught).

1930. Arranges a joint exhibition in his studio with Roy de Maistre, showing furniture as well as paintings and gouaches. *The Studio* magazine features a double-page article on his studio entitled ''The 1930 Look in British Decoration''.

1931. Moves to the Fulham Road. Gradually abandons his work as a decorator in order to devote himself to painting. Earns his living by doing odd jobs, none of them connected with art.

1933. Paints *Crucifixion 1933*, which is reproduced in Herbert Read's *Art Now*.

1936. Submits some work to the International Surrealist Exhibition. It is rejected as ''not sufficiently surreal''.

1937. Takes part in an important group exhibition, ''Young British Painters'', at Agnews, London, organized by his friend Eric Hall. Other artists include Roy de Maistre, Graham Sutherland, Victor Pasmore and Ivon Hitchens.

1941-44. Moves for a short time to a cottage in Petersfield, Hampshire. Returns to London and rents Millais's old studio in Kensington. Destroys nearly all his earlier works (only ten canvases remain from the period 1929-44). Declared unfit for military service because of his asthma, is assigned to Civil Defense (ARP).

1944-45. Resumes painting in earnest and executes the triptych *Three Studies for Figures at the Base of a Crucifixion*, which causes considerable consternation when shown at the Lefevre Gallery in April 1945. The mysterious forms were regarded as freaks, monsters irrelevant to the concerns of the day, and the product of an imagination so eccentric as not to count in any permanent way. The triptych is acquired by the Tate Gallery in 1953.

1945-46. Exhibits *Figure in a Landscape* and *Figure Study II* in group exhibitions held at the Lefevre and Redfern Galleries. Other artists include Matthew Smith, Henry Moore and Graham Sutherland.

1946-50. Lives mainly in Monte Carlo. Friendship with Graham Sutherland.

1948. Alfred H. Barr purchases *Painting 1946*, one of his most important works, for the Museum of Modern Art, New York.

1949. One-man show at the Hanover Gallery, London, who become his agents for the next ten years. Begins painting the series of Heads (including *Head VI*, which is regarded as the first of the ''Pope'' paintings and *Head IV (Man with Monkey)*. Uses Eadweard Muybridge's photographic studies *Animal Locomotion* and *Human Figure in Motion* as a source of reference for his paintings of animals and the human figure.

1950. Teaches briefly at the Royal College of Art as deputy for John Minton. Travels to South Africa to visit his mother; spends a few days in Cairo.

1951-55. Changes studios several times.

1953. First one-man show outside Britain at Durlacher Brothers, New York. Paints *Two Figures* (The Wrestlers), considered by many as one of his greatest paintings.

1954. Paints the *Man in Blue* series. Together with Ben Nicholson and Lucian Freud, represents Great Britain at the XXVII Venice Biennale. Takes opportunity to visit Ostia and Rome but does not attend the Biennale or see the Velázquez portrait of *Pope Innocent X*, the reproduction of which inspired his series of ''Popes''.

1955. First retrospective exhibition at the Institute of Contemporary Arts, London. Paints portraits of the collectors Robert and Lisa Sainsbury, who become his patrons.

1956. Visits Tangier to see his friend Peter Lacey. Rents a flat and returns there frequently during the next three years.

1957. First exhibition in Paris, at the Galerie Rive Droite. Exhibits the Van Gogh Series at the Hanover Gallery, London.

1958. First one-man exhibitions in Italy; shows in Turin, Milan and Rome. Signs contract with Marlborough Fine Art Ltd., London.

1959. Exhibition at the V São Paulo Biennale.
Paints for a while in St. Ives, Cornwall.

1960. First exhibition at Marlborough Fine Art, London.

1962. Paints his first large triptych, *Three Studies for a Crucifixion*, acquired by the Solomon R. Guggenheim Museum, New York. Major retrospective exhibition at the Tate Gallery, London. Modified version shown in Mannheim, Turin and Zurich (1963). Death of Peter Lacey.

1963-64. Retrospective exhibition at the Solomon R. Guggenheim Museum, New York, and afterwards at the Art Institute of Chicago.

1964. Friendship with George Dyer, who becomes a model for many of his paintings. Executes large Triptych, *3 Figures in a Room*, acquired by the Musée National d'Art Moderne, Paris.

1965. Paints large *Crucifixion* triptych, acquired by Munich Museum.

1966. Awarded the Rubens Prize by the City of Siegen. Exhibits at the Galerie Maeght, Paris. The artist attends the opening. The exhibition travels to Marlborough Fine Art, London (1967).

1967. Awarded the Painting Prize at the 1967 Pittsburgh International.

1968. Short visit to New York for exhibition of his recent paintings at the Marlborough-Gerson Gallery.

1971-72. Important retrospective exhibition at the Grand Palais, Paris; subsequently shown at the Kunsthalle, Dusseldorf.
Death in Paris of his friend and model George Dyer (1971).
Paints large *Triptych 1971* in his memory.

1975. Travels to New York to attend Opening of his major Exhibition at the Metropolitan Museum of Art.

1977. Visits Paris for Private View of his Exhibition at Galerie Claude Bernard.

1978. Brief visit to Rome to meet Balthus at the Villa Medici.

1980. The Tate Gallery acquires *Triptych - August* 1972.

1984. Short visit to New York for his Exhibition of recent work at Marlborough Gallery.

1985-86. Second Retrospective Exhibition at the Tate Gallery (125 works) which travels to Staatsgalerie Stuttgart and Nationalgalerie Berlin. Visits Berlin with his friend John Edwards. Paints large self portrait triptych.

1987. Francis Bacon lives and work in London — with occasional visits to France.

BIBLIOGRAPHY

MONOGRAPHS

1964
Rothenstein, Sir John, and Alley, Ronald, *Francis Bacon*, Catalogue Raisonné, Thames and Hudson, London. 292 pp. illus.

Russell, John, *Francis Bacon*, Series "Art in Progress", Methuen & Co., London. 26 pp. illus.

1963-67
Rothenstein, Sir John, *Francis Bacon*, The Masters, Fratelli Fabbri, Milan 1963; Purnell and Sons. Ltd., London, No. 71, 244 pp. illus.; Hachette, Paris, 1967, 12 pp. illus.

1971
Russell, John, *Francis Bacon*, Thames and Hudson, London; Les Éditions du Chêne, Paris; Propylaën Verlag, Berlin. 242 pp. illus.

1974
Leiris, Michel, *Francis Bacon ou la Vérité criante*, Éditions Fata Morgana, Paris.

1975
Sylvester, David, *Interviews with Francis Bacon*, Thames and Hudson, London and Pantheon Books Inc., New York, 128 pp. illus.; *L'Art de l'impossible* (French edition of Interviews by David Sylvester). Preface by Michel Leiris, Series "Les Sentiers de la Creation", Editions Albert Skira, Geneva 1976; *Entrevistas con Francis Bacon* (Spanish edition), Ediciones Polígrafa, S. A., Barcelona, 1977; *Samtal med Francis Bacon* (Swedish edition), Forum Stockholm 1977. New enlarged edition published by Thames and Hudson, London, 1980. *Gespräche mit Francis Bacon* (German edition), Prestel Verlag, Munich, 1982. Thames and Hudson, New York, 1985.

Trucchi, Lorenza, *Francis Bacon*, Fratelli Fabbri Editori, Milan, 1975; English Edition, Thames and Hudson, London, and Abrams, New York, 1976. New revised edition published by Fratelli Fabbri Editori, Milan, 1984.

1978
Bacon Opus International No. 68, Editions George Fall, Paris.

1979
Russell, John, *Francis Bacon* (revised edition), World of Art Series, Thames and Hudson, London, Oxford University Press, New York, 192 pp. illus.

1981
Deleuze, Gilles, *Francis Bacon, Logique de la Sensation*, Éditions de la Différence, Paris, 2 vols. 112 pp. and 164 pp. illus. New enlarged edition, published by Editions de la Difference, Paris, 1984.

1983
Leiris, Michel, *Francis Bacon, Full Face and in Profile*; English Edition, Phaidon, London and Rizzoli, New York; Frech Edition, Albin Michel, Paris; German Edition, Prestel Verlag, Munich; Italian Edition, Rizzoli, Milan; Spanish Edition, Poligrafa, Barcelona, 272 pp., 240 colour illus.

1985.
Ades, Dawn and Forge, Andrew, *Francis Bacon*, Thames and Hudson, London, published in association with The Tate Gallery, London, 246 pp., 195 colour illus.

Schmied, Wieland, *Francis Bacon: Vier Studien zu einem Porträt*, Frolich & Kaufmann, Berlin, 164 pp. illus.

1986.
Zimmerman, Jörg, *Francis Bacon: Kreuzigung*, Fischer Taschenbuch Verlag GmbH, Frankfurt am Main, 101 pp., ilus.

Davies, Hugh and Yard, Sally, *Francis Bacon*, Abbeville Press, New York, 128 pp., illus.

FILMS

1962-63
Francis Bacon: Paintings 1944-62, conceived and directed by David Thompson, music by Elizabeth Lutyens. Film made for the Arts Council of Great Britain and Marlborough Fine Art (Ltd.), by Samaritan Films, London. Distributed by Gala Films.

1966
Sunday Night Francis Bacon. Interviews with David Sylvester, directed by Michael Gill for BBC Television, London. Extracts reproduced in catalogue *Bacon* exhibition, Marlborough Fine Art (Ltd.), London, 1967.

1971
Francis Bacon. Interview with Maurice Chapuis, directed by J. M. Berzosa for ORTF Television, Paris. Film made in connection with Bacon retrospective exhibition at the Grand Palais, Paris, 1971.

Review - Francis Bacon, produced by Colin Nears, directed by Gavin Millar, for BBC Television, London. Film made in connection with the Bacon retrospective exhibition at the Grand Palais, Paris, 1971.

1974
Portrait of Francis Bacon, directed by Thomas Ayck for NDR Television, Hamburg.

1975
Interviews with Bacon by David Sylvester, Aquarius, London Weekend Television.

1983
Regards Entendus Francis Bacon. Text by Michel Leiris, produced by Constantin Jelenski, Institut National de l'Audiovisuel, Bry-sur-Marne, French Television.

1984
Après Hiroshima ... Francis Bacon? Interview with Pierre Daix for French Television Programme *Désirs des Arts*. Film made in connection with Francis Bacon exhibition of recent paintings at the Galerie Maeght, Paris, 1984.

The Brutality of Fact. *Interview with David Sylvester. Directed by Michael Blackwood and produced by Alan Yentob for Arena* BBC Television, London.

1985
Francis Bacon. Interview with Melvyn Bragg for the *South Bank Show*, London Weekend Television.

PUBLIC COLLECTIONS

AUSTRALIA
Adelaide   National Gallery of South Australia
Brisbane   Queensland Art Gallery
Canberra   National Gallery of Australia
Melbourne   The National Gallery of Victoria
Sydney   Art Gallery of New South Wales

AUSTRIA
Vienna   Museum Moderner Kunst

BELGIUM
Brussels   Musées Royaux des Beaux-Arts de Belgique
Ghent   Musée des Beaux-Arts
Liège   Musée des Beaux-Arts

CANADA
Ottawa   The National Gallery of Canada

DENMARK
Humlebaek   Louisiana Museum of Modern Art

FINLAND
Helsinki   Art Museum Atheneum
Tampere   Sara Hildén Art Museum

FRANCE
Marseille   Musée Cantini
Paris   Musée National d'Art Moderne, Centre
    Georges Pompidou

GERMANY
Berlin   Nationalgalerie
Bochum   Städtische Kunstgalerie
Cologne   Wallraf-Richartz Museum, Ludwig Collection
Düsseldorf   Kunstsammlung Nordrhein-Westfalen
Frankfurt   Städelsches Kunstinstitut
    Museum für Moderner Kunst
Hamburg   Kunsthalle
Hanover   Kunstmuseum
Mannheim   Kunsthalle
Munich   Staatsgalerie Modern Kunst
Stuttgart   Staatsgalerie
Wuppertal   Von der Heydt Museum

GREAT BRITAIN
& N. IRELAND
Aberdeen   Art Gallery
Belfast   Ulster Museum
Birmingham   City Art Gallery
Cardiff   National Museum of Wales
Huddersfield   Art Gallery, Kirkless Metropolitan Council
Leeds   Temple Newsam House
Leicester   Museums and Art Gallery
London   The Arts Council of Great Britain
    Royal College of Art
    The Tate Gallery
    Victoria & Albert Museum
Manchester   City Art Gallery
    Whitworth Art Gallery

Newcastle-
upon-Tyne   King's College Hatton Gallery
Norwich   University of East Anglia
Oxford   Pembroke College

ISRAEL
Jerusalem   Bezalel National Museum

ITALY
Milan   Brera Museum of Modern Art
Rome   Vatican Museum of Modern Art
Turin   Galleria Civica d'Arte Moderna

JAPAN
Fukuoka   Museum of Art
Ito   Ikeda Museum 20th Century Art
Nagaoka   Contemporary Art Museum
Tokyo   National Museum of Modern Art
Toyama   Museum of Modern Art

MEXICO
Mexico City   Museo Rufino Tamayo

NETHERLANDS
Amsterdam   Stedelijk Museum
Eindhoven   Stedelijk Van Abbe Museum
The Hague   Gemeentemuseum
Rotterdam   Boymans Van Beuningen Museum

SPAIN
Bilbao   Museo de Bellas Artes
Madrid   Museo Español de Arte Contemporáneo

SWEDEN
Gothenburg   Art Gallery
Stockholm   Moderna Museet

SWITZERLAND
Zürich   Kunsthaus

U.S.A.
Buffalo   Albright Knox Art Gallery
Chicago   The Art Institute
    Institute of Contemporary Art
Cleveland   Museum of Art
Dallas   Museum of Fine Art
Des Moines   Art Center
Detroit   Institute of Arts
Hawaii   Honolulu Academy of Arts
Minneapolis   Institute of Arts
New Haven   Yale University Art Gallery
New York   The Solomon R. Guggenheim Museum
    Museum of Modern Art
Omaha   Joslyn Art Museum
Poughkeepsie   Vassar College Art Gallery
Washington   The Joseph H. Hirshhorn Museum &
    Sculpture Garden
    Phillips Collection

VENEZUELA
Caracas   Museo de Arte Contemporáneo

ILLUSTRATIONS

1
Three Studies for Figures at
the Base of a Crucifixion. 1944.
Oil and pastel on hardboard,
each panel 37 × 29 in. / 94 × 74 cm.
The Tate Gallery, London.

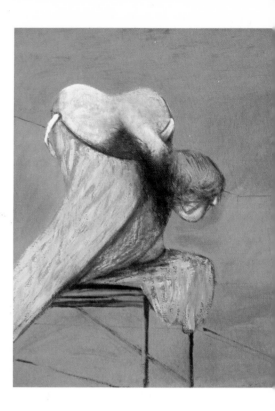

2
Figure in a Landscape. 1945.
Oil on canvas,
57 × 50 ½ in. / 145 × 128 cm.
The Tate Gallery, London.

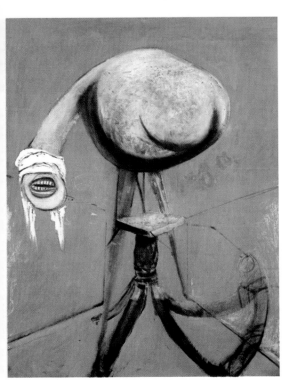

3
Figure Study I. 1945-46.
Oil on canvas,
48 ½ × 41 ½ in. / 123 × 105.5 cm.
Private collection.

Left

4
Painting. 1946.
Oil and tempera on canvas,
78 × 52 in. / 198 × 132 cm.
The Museum of Modern Art, New York.

5
Study from the Human Body. 1949.
Oil on canvas,
58 × 51 ½ in. / 147.5 × 131 cm.
The National Gallery of Victoria, Melbourne
(Felton Bequest).

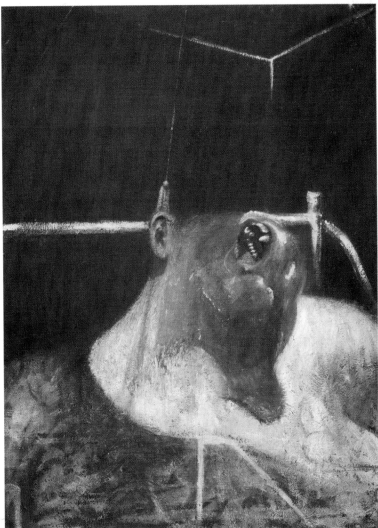

6
Head I. 1948.
Oil and tempera on board,
40 ½ × 29 ½ in. / 103 × 75 cm.
Collection Richard S. Zeisler, New York.

7
Head VI. 1949.
Oil on canvas,
36¾ × 30¼ in. / 93 × 77 cm.
The Arts Council of Great Britain, London.

8
Head III. 1949.
Oil on canvas,
32 × 26 in. / 81 × 66 cm.
Private collection.

Right

9
Study for Crouching Nude. 1952.
Oil on canvas,
78 × 54 in. / 198 × 137 cm.
The Detroit Institute of Arts
(Gift of Dr. Wilhelm R. Valentiner).

10
Three Studies of the Human Head. 1953.
Triptych.
Oil on canvas,
each panel 24 × 20 in. / 61 × 51 cm.
Private collection.

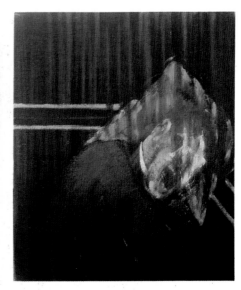

11
Study for a Portrait. 1953.
Oil on canvas,
60 × 46 ½ in. / 152.5 × 118 cm.
Kunsthalle, Hamburg.

12
Study after Velázquez's Portrait of
Pope Innocent X. 1953.
Oil on canvas,
60 ¼ × 46 ½ in. / 153 × 118 cm.
Des Moines Art Center,
Coffin Fine Arts Trust Fund, 1980.

13
Dog. 1952.
Oil on canvas,
78 ¼ × 54 ¼ in. / 199 × 138 cm.
The Museum of Modern Art, New York.

14
Chimpanzee. 1955.
Oil on canvas,
60 × 46 in. / 152.5 × 117 cm.
Staatsgalerie, Stuttgart.

15
Man with Dog. 1953.
Oil on canvas,
59 ⅞ × 46 in. / 152 × 117 cm.
Albright-Knox Art Gallery, Buffalo, New York
(Gift of Seymour H. Knox, 1955).

16
Two Figures. 1953.
Oil on canvas,
60 × 45 ⅞ in. / 152.5 × 116.5 cm.
Private collection.

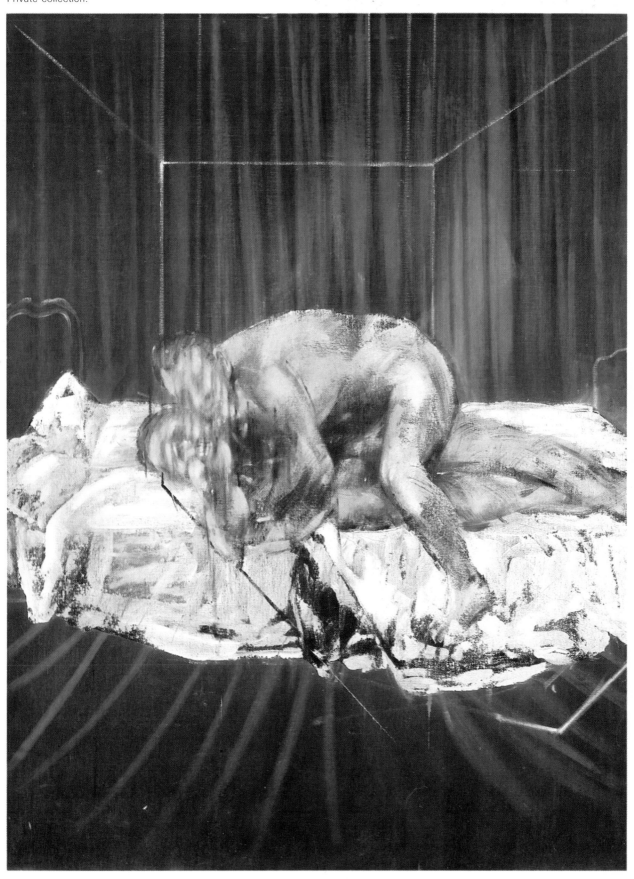

17
Study for Portrait of Van Gogh II. 1957.
Oil on canvas,
78×56 in. / 198×142 cm.
Collection Edwin Janss, Thousand Oaks, California.

18
Study for Portrait of Van Gogh VI. 1957.
Oil on canvas,
79¾×56 in. / 202.5×142 cm.
The Arts Council of Great Britain, London.

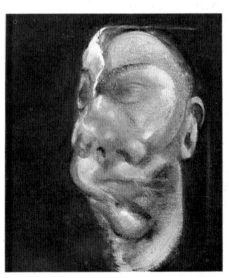

19
Study for Three Heads. 1962.
Small triptych.
Oil on canvas,
each panel 14×12 in. / 35.5×30.5 cm.
Collection William S. Paley, New York.

Right

20
Study from Innocent X. 1962.
Oil on canvas,
78×57⅛ in. / 198×145 cm.
Collection M. Riklis.

21
Three Studies for a Crucifixion. 1962.
Triptych.
Oil on canvas,
each panel 78 × 57 in. / 198 × 145 cm.
The Solomon R. Guggenheim Museum, New York.

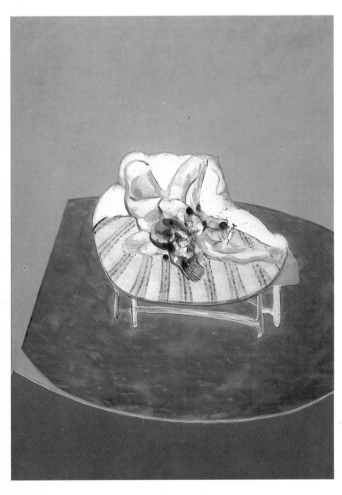

22
Lying Figure with Hypodermic Syringe. 1963.
Oil on canvas,
78 × 57 in. / 198 × 145 cm.
Private collection, Switzerland.

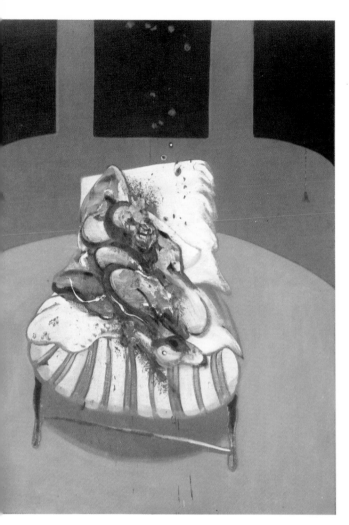

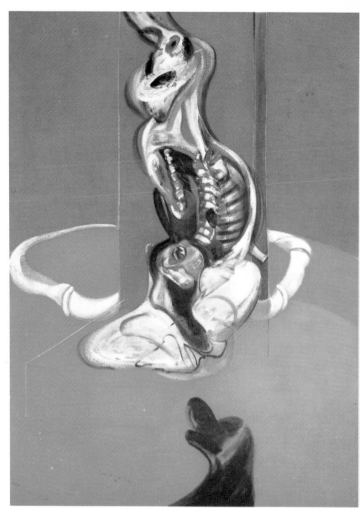

23
Three Studies for Portrait of George Dyer
(on light ground). 1964.
Small triptych.
Oil on canvas,
each panel 14 × 12 in. / 35.5 × 30.5 cm.
Private collection.

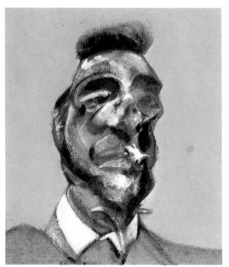

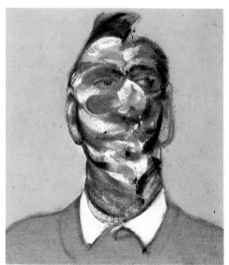

24
Double Portrait of Lucian Freud and
Frank Auerbach. 1964.
Diptych.
Oil on canvas,
each panel 65 × 56⅞ in. / 165 × 145 cm.
Moderna Museet, Stockholm.

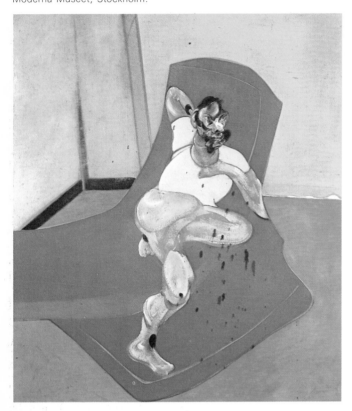

25
Three Studies for Head of Isabel
Rawsthorne. 1965.
Small triptych.
Oil on canvas,
each panel 14 × 12 in. / 35.5 × 30.5 cm.
Robert and Lisa Sainsbury Collection,
University of East Anglia, Norwich.

26
Study for Portrait (Isabel Rawsthorne). 1964.
Oil on canvas,
78 × 58 in. / 198 × 147.5 cm.
Private collection.

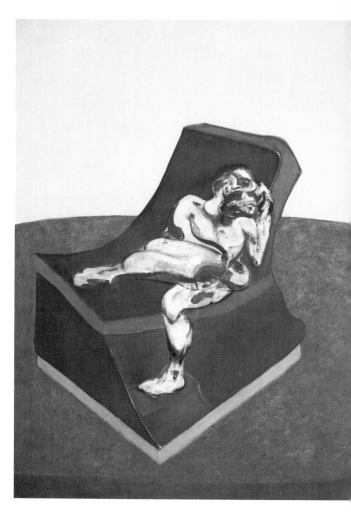

27
Three Figures in a Room. 1964.
Triptych.
Oil on canvas,
each panel 78 × 57 ⅞ in. / 198 × 147 cm.
Musée National d'Art Moderne,
Centre Georges Pompidou, Paris.

28
Three Studies for Portrait of Lucian Freud. 1965.
Small triptych.
Oil on canvas,
each panel 14 × 12 in. / 35.5 × 30.5 cm.
Private collection.

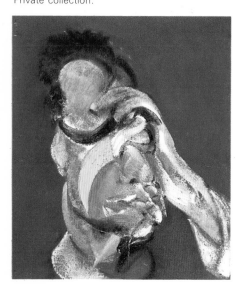

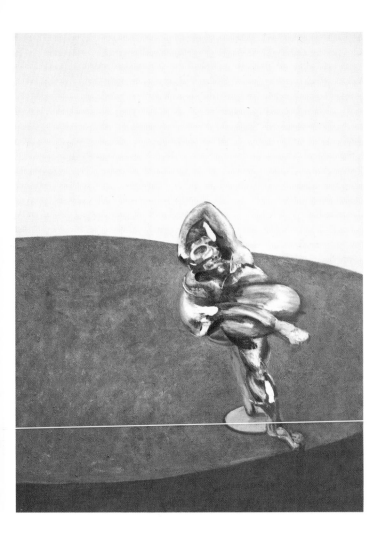

29
Portrait of Lucian Freud (on Orange Couch). 1965.
Oil on canvas,
61 ½ × 54 ¾ in. / 156 × 139 cm.
Private collection.

30
Crucifixion. 1965.
Triptych.
Oil on canvas,
each panel 77⅝ × 57⅞ in. / 197.2 × 147 cm.
Staatsgalerie Moderner Kunst, Munich
(Gift of the Galerie-Vereins, Munich eV).

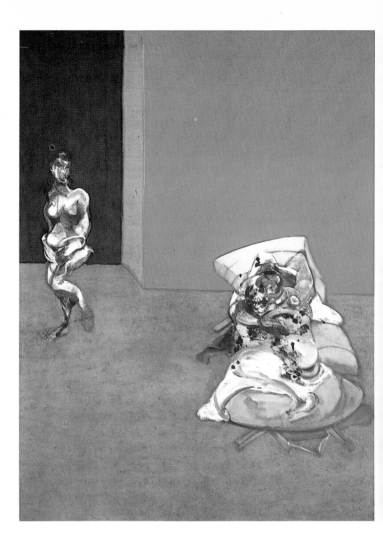

31
**After Muybridge — Study of the Human Figure in
Motion — Woman Emptying a Bowl of Water,
and Paralytic Child on All Fours.** 1965.
Oil on canvas,
78 × 58 in. / 198 × 147.5 cm.
Stedelijk Museum, Amsterdam.

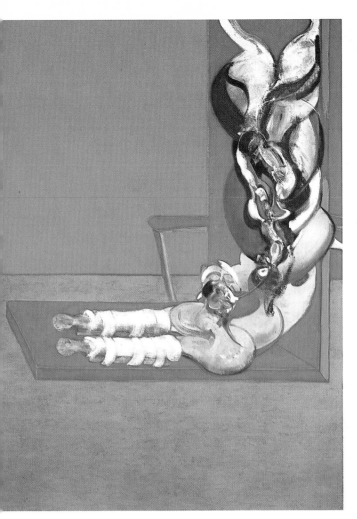

32
Three Studies of Isabel Rawsthorne
(on White Ground). 1965.
Small triptych.
Oil on canvas,
each panel 14 × 12 in. / 35.5 × 30.5 cm.
Private collection.

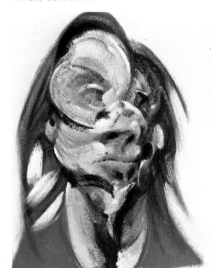

33
**Three Studies of Isabel Rawsthorne
(on Light Ground).** 1965.
Small triptych.
Oil on canvas,
each panel 14 × 12 in. / 35.5 × 30.5 cm.
Private collection.

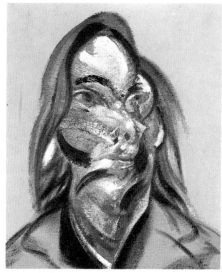

34
Three Studies of Isabel Rawsthorne. 1966.
Small triptych.
Oil on canvas,
each panel 14 × 12 in. / 35.5 × 30.5 cm.
Private collection, Paris.

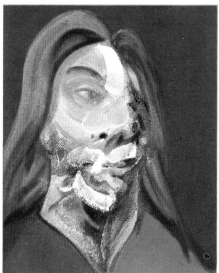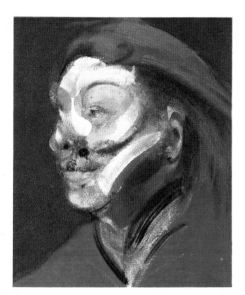

35
Study of Isabel Rawsthorne. 1966.
Oil on canvas,
14 × 12 in. / 35.5 × 30.5 cm.
Louise and Michel Leiris Collection, Paris.

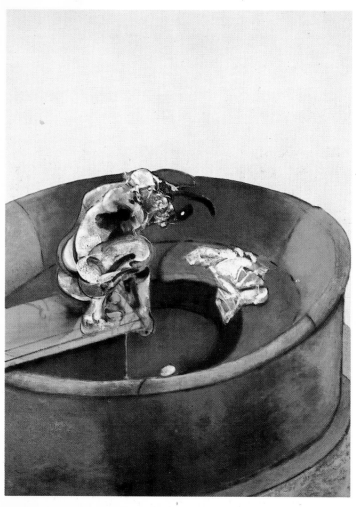

36
Portrait of George Dyer Crouching. 1966.
Oil on canvas,
78 × 58 in. / 198 × 147.5 cm.
Private collection, Caracas.

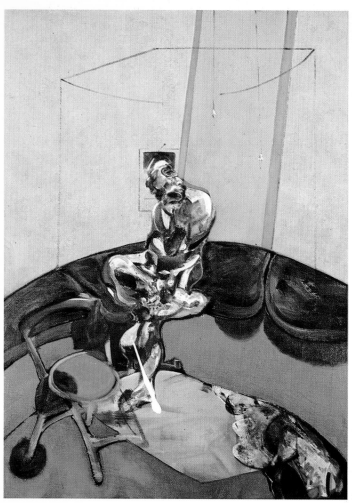

37
Portrait of George Dyer Staring at Blind Cord. 1966.
Oil on canvas,
78 × 58 in. / 198 × 147.5 cm.
Private collection.

38
Portrait of George Dyer Talking. 1966.
Oil on canvas,
78 × 58 in. / 198 × 147.5 cm.
Private collection, New York.

39
Three Studies for Portrait of Lucian Freud. 1966.
Triptych.
Oil on canvas,
each panel 78 × 58 in. / 198 × 147.5 cm.
Marlborough International Fine Art.

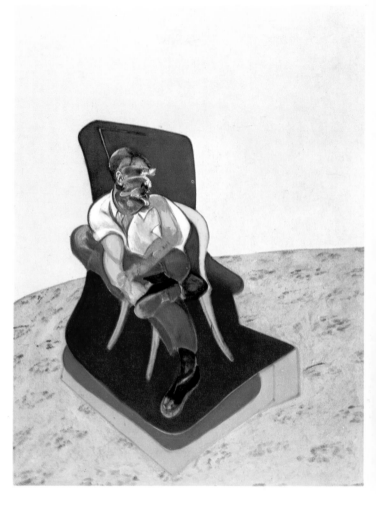

40
Lying Figure. 1966.
Oil on canvas,
78 × 58 in. / 198 × 147.5 cm.
Museo Español de Arte Contemporáneo, Madrid.

41
Three Studies of Muriel Belcher. 1966.
Small triptych.
Oil on canvas,
each panel 14 × 12 in. / 35.5 × 30.5 cm.
Private collection.

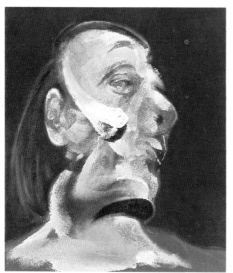
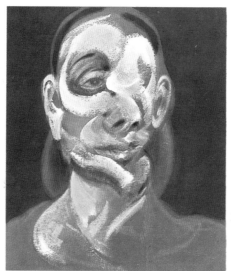
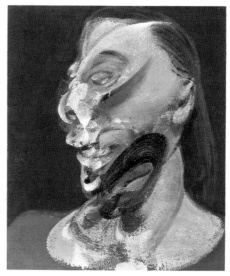

42
Three Studies of George Dyer. 1966.
Small triptych.
Oil on canvas,
each panel 14 × 12 in. / 35.5 × 30.5 cm.
Private collection, New York.

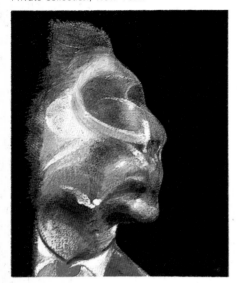  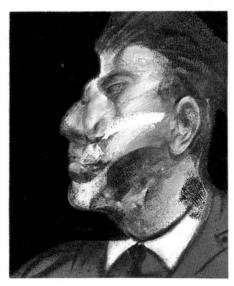

43
Study for Head of George Dyer. 1967.
Oil on canvas,
14 × 12 in. / 35.5 × 30.5 cm.
Private collection.

Right

44
**Portrait of George Dyer
Riding a Bicycle.** 1966.
Oil on canvas,
78 × 58 in. / 198 × 147.5 cm.
Galerie Beyeler, Basle.

45
Study for Head of George Dyer and Isabel Rawsthorne. 1967.
Diptych.
Oil on canvas,
each panel 14 × 12 in. / 35.5 × 30.5 cm.
Private collection, Italy.

46
Three Studies of Isabel Rawsthorne. 1967.
Oil on canvas,
46⅞ × 60 in. / 119 × 152.5 cm.
Staatliche Museen Preussischer Kulturbesitz,
Nationalgalerie, Berlin.

47
Portrait of Isabel Rawsthorne. 1966.
Oil on canvas,
26¾ × 18⅛ in. / 67 × 46 cm.
The Tate Gallery, London.

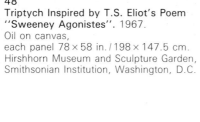

48
Triptych Inspired by T.S. Eliot's Poem
''Sweeney Agonistes''. 1967.
Oil on canvas,
each panel 78 × 58 in. / 198 × 147.5 cm.
Hirshhorn Museum and Sculpture Garden,
Smithsonian Institution, Washington, D.C.

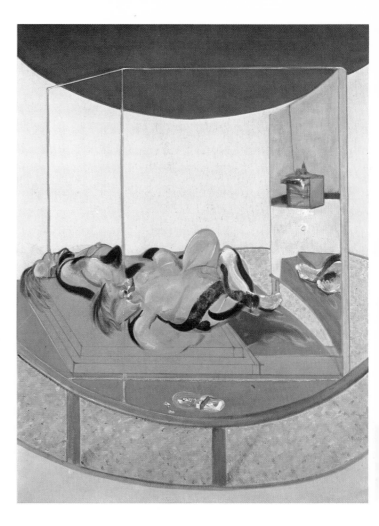

49
Portrait of Isabel Rawsthorne Standing in a
Street in Soho. 1967.
Oil on canvas,
78 × 58 in. / 198 × 147.5 cm.
Staatliche Museen Preussischer Kulturbesitz,
Nationalgalerie, Berlin.

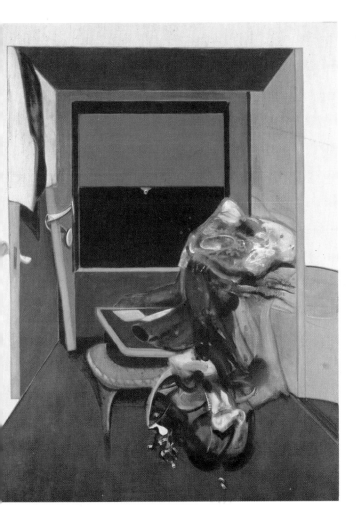

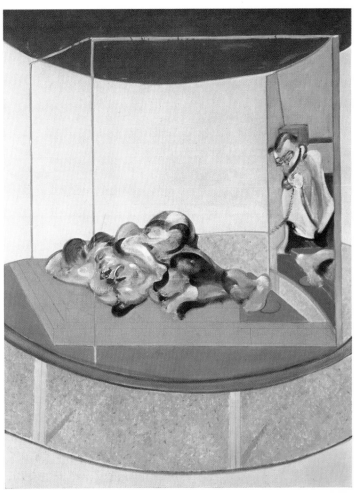

50
Three Studies of Isabel Rawsthorne. 1968.
Small triptych.
Oil on canvas,
each panel 14 × 12 in. / 35.5 × 30.5 cm.
Mrs Susan Lloyd Collection, Nassau.

51
Portrait of George Dyer in a Mirror. 1968.
Oil on canvas,
78 × 58 in. / 198 × 147.5 cm.
Thyssen-Bornemisza Collection, Lugano, Switzerland.

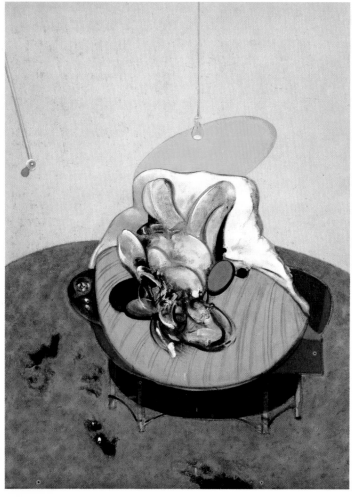

52
Lying Figure. 1969.
Oil on canvas,
78 × 58 in. / 198 × 147.5 cm.
Galerie Beyeler, Basle.

53
Three Studies for Portrait. 1968.
Small triptych.
Oil on canvas,
each panel 14 × 12 in. / 35.5 × 30.5 cm.
Private collection.

54
Two Studies of George Dyer with Dog. 1968.
Oil on canvas,
78 × 58 in. / 198 × 147.5 cm.
Private collection.

55
Two Studies for a Portrait of George Dyer. 1968.
Oil on canvas,
78 × 58 in. / 198 × 147.5 cm.
Sara Hildén Foundation,
Sara Hildén Art Museum, Tampere, Finland.

56
Two Figures Lying on a Bed with Attendants. 1968.
Triptych.
Oil on canvas,
each panel 78 × 58 in. / 198 × 147.5 cm.
Present whereabouts unknown.

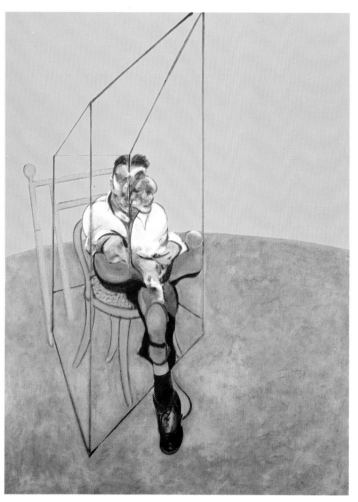

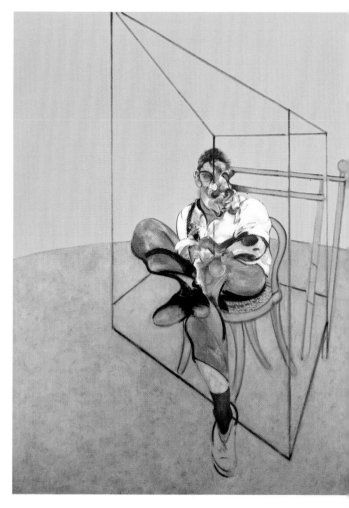

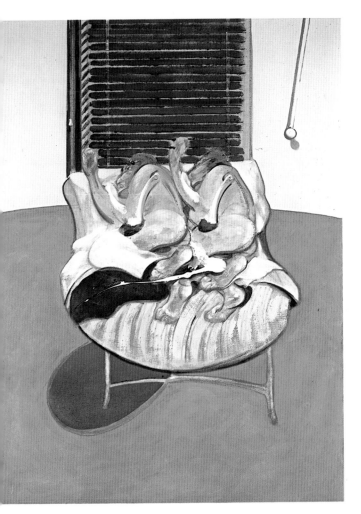

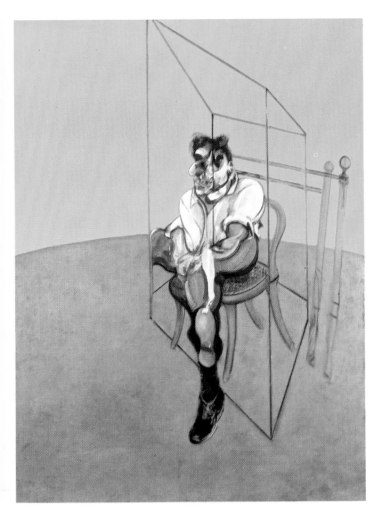

57
Three Studies of Lucian Freud. 1969.
Triptych.
Oil on canvas,
each panel 78 × 58 in. / 198 × 147.5 cm.
Private collection, Rome.

58

Three Studies of Henrietta Moraes. 1969.
Small triptych.
Oil on canvas,
each panel 14 × 12 in. / 35.5 × 30.5 cm.
Capricorn Art International, S. A. Collection, Panama.

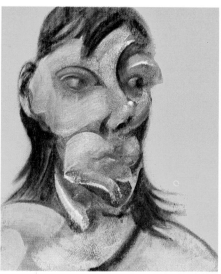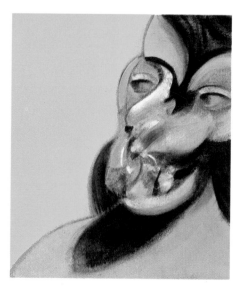

59

Three Studies of Henrietta Moraes. 1969.
Small triptych.
Oil on canvas,
each panel 14 × 12 in. / 35.5 × 30.5 cm.
Gilbert de Botton Collection, Switzerland.

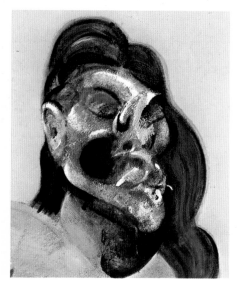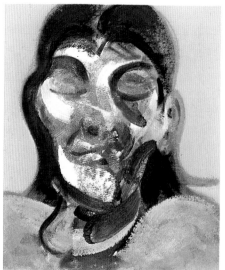

60
Study of Henrietta Moraes Laughing. 1969.
Oil on canvas,
14 × 12 in. / 35.5 × 30.5 cm.
Private collection.

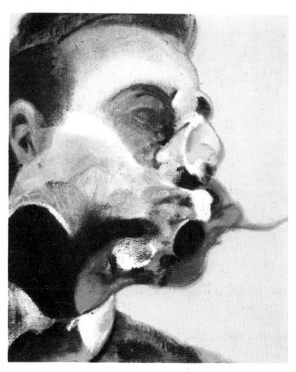

61
Studies of George Dyer and Isabel Rawsthorne. 1970.
Diptych.
Oil on canvas,
each panel 14 × 12 in. / 35.5 × 30.5 cm.
Private collection.

62
Three Studies of George Dyer. 1969.
Small triptych.
Oil on canvas,
each panel 14 × 12 in. / 35.5 × 30.5 cm.
Louisiana Museum, Humlebaek.

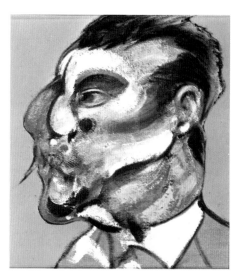

64
Study for Bullfight No. 1. 1969.
Oil on canvas,
78 × 58 in. / 198 × 147.5 cm.
Private collection.

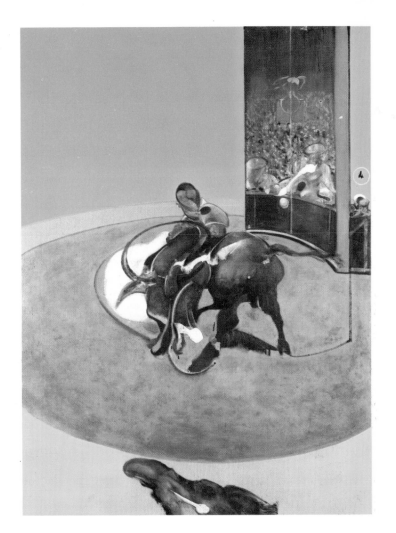

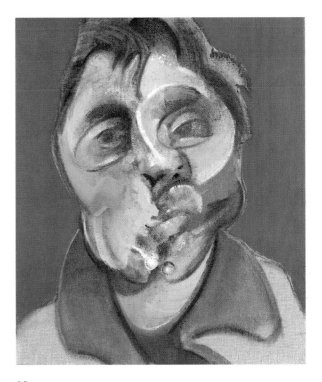

63
Self-Portrait. 1969.
Oil on canvas,
14 × 12 in. / 35.5 × 30.5 cm.
Private collection, London.

65
Second Version of "Study for Bullfight No. 1". 1969.
Oil on canvas,
78 × 58 in. / 198 × 147.5 cm.
Galerie Beyeler, Basle.

66
Three Studies of the Male Back. 1970.
Triptych.
Oil on canvas,
each panel 78 × 58 in. / 198 × 147.5 cm.
Kunsthaus, Zürich. Vereinigung Zürcher Kunstfreunde.

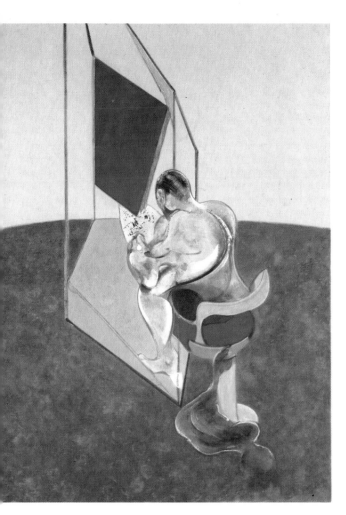

67
Studies of the Human Body. 1970.
Triptych.
Oil on canvas,
each panel 78 × 58 in. / 198 × 147.5 cm.
Marlborough International Fine Art.

68
Studies of the Human Body. 1970.
Triptych.
Oil on canvas,
each panel 78 × 58 in. / 198 × 147.5 cm.
Jacques Hachuel Collection.

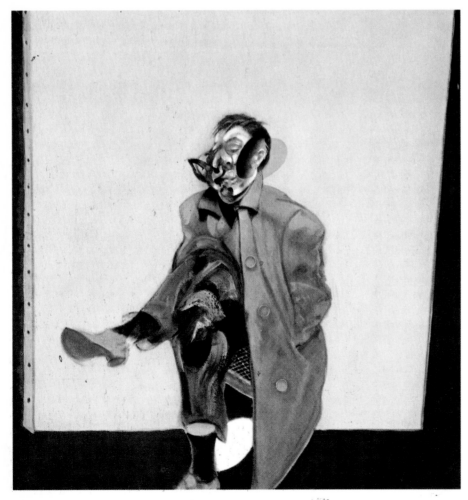

69
Self-Portrait. 1970.
Oil on canvas,
59⅞ × 58 in. / 152 × 147.5 cm.
Private collection.

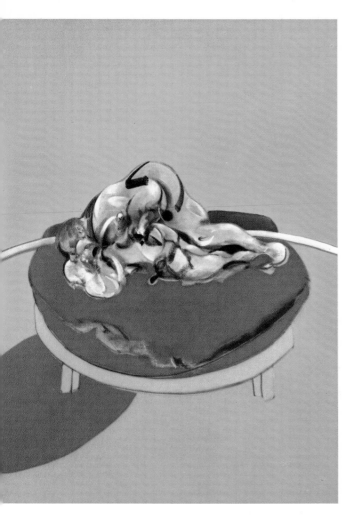

70
Study for Portrait. 1970.
Oil on canvas,
78 × 58 in. / 198 × 147.5 cm.
Private collection, France.

71
Study for Portrait. 1971.
Oil on canvas,
78 × 58 in. / 198 × 147.5 cm.
Private collection, London.

72
Second version of ''Painting 1946''. 1971.
Oil on canvas,
78 × 58 in. / 198 × 147.5 cm.
Ludwig Museum, Cologne.

73
Triptych. 1971.
Oil on canvas,
each panel 78 × 58 in. / 198 × 147.5 cm.
Galerie Beyeler, Basle.

74
Female Nude Standing in a Doorway. 1972.
Oil on canvas,
78 × 58 in. / 198 × 147.5 cm.
Private collection, France.

75
Study for Portrait of Lucian Freud (Sideways).
August, 1971.
Oil on canvas,
78 × 58 in. / 198 × 147.5 cm.
Private collection, London.

76

Three Studies for Self-Portrait. 1972.
Small triptych.
Oil on canvas,
each panel 14 × 12 in. / 35.5 × 30.5 cm.
Private collection.

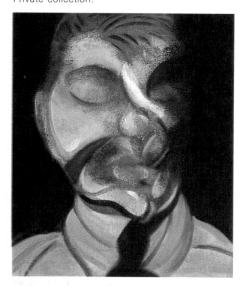  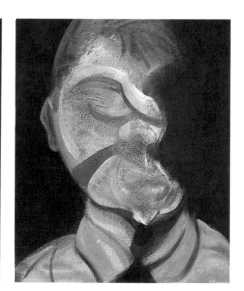

77
Self-Portrait. 1971.
Oil on canvas,
14 × 12 in. / 35.5 × 30.5 cm.
Louise and Michel Leiris Collection, Paris.

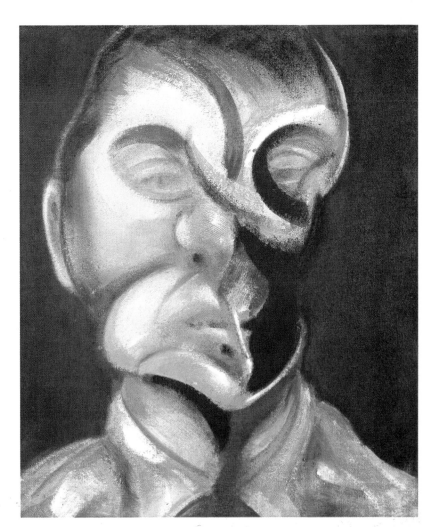

78
Self-Portrait. 1972.
Oil on canvas,
14 × 12 in. / 35.5 × 30.5 cm.
Private collection.

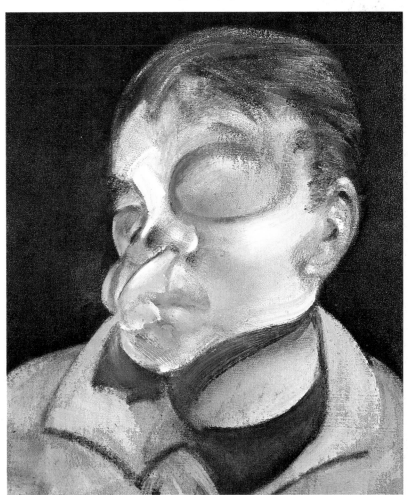

79
**Self-Portrait with
Injured Eye.** 1972.
Oil on canvas,
14 × 12 in. / 35.5 × 30.5 cm.
Private collection.

80
Three Studies of Figures on Beds. 1972.
Triptych.
Oil and pastel on canvas,
each panel 78 × 58 in. / 198 × 147.5 cm.
Private collection.

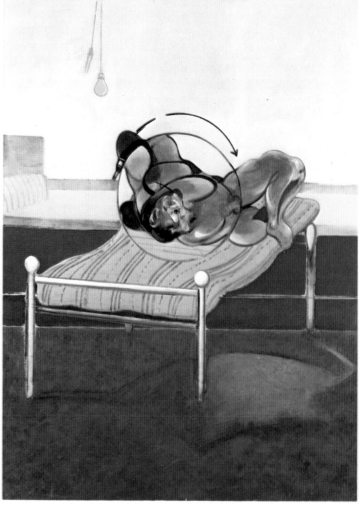

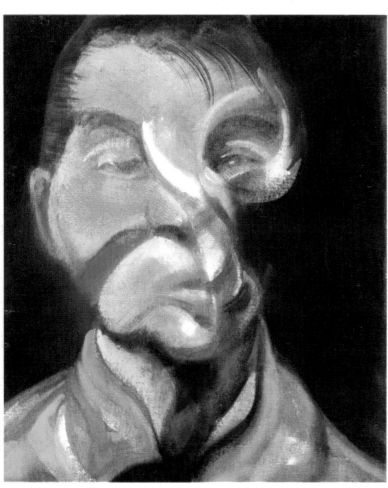

81
Self-Portrait. 1972.
Oil on canvas,
14 × 12 in. / 35.5 × 30.5 cm.
Gilbert de Botton Collection, Switzerland.

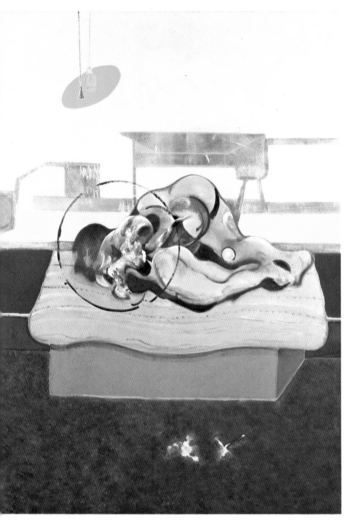
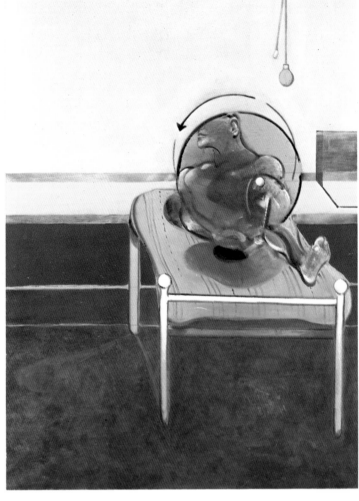

82
Three Studies for Self-Portrait. 1973.
Small triptych.
Oil on canvas,
each panel 14 × 12 in. / 35.5 × 30.5 cm.
Private collection.

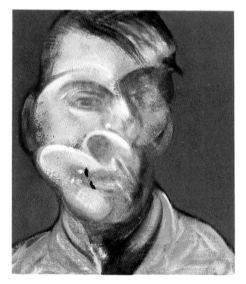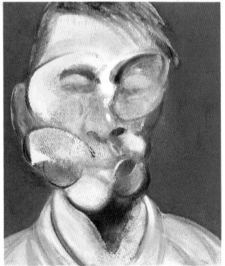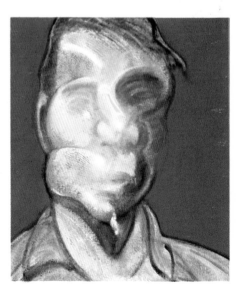

83
Triptych. **August.** 1972.
Oil on canvas,
each panel 78 × 58 in. / 198 × 147.5 cm.
The Tate Gallery, London.

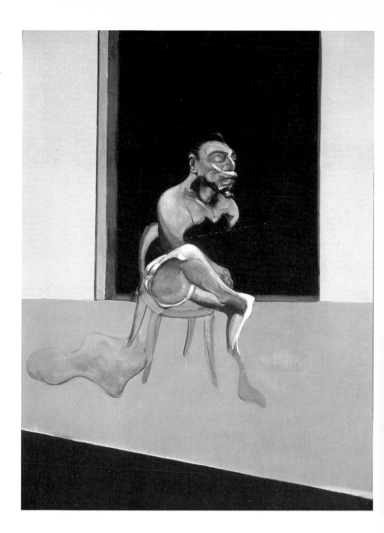

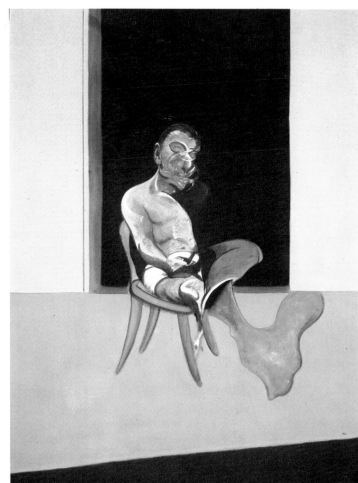

84
Triptych. May-June. 1973.
Oil on canvas,
each panel 78 × 58 in. / 198 × 147.5 cm.
Mr and Mrs Saul P. Steinberg Collection.

85
Self-Portrait. 1972.
Oil on canvas,
78 × 58 in. / 198 × 147.5 cm.
Private collection.

86
Self-Portrait. 1973.
Oil on canvas,
78 × 58 in. / 198 × 147.5 cm.
Private collection.

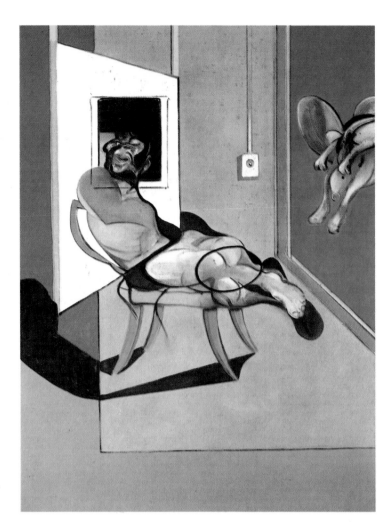

87
Seated Figure. 1974.
Oil and pastel on canvas,
78 × 58 in. / 198 × 147.5 cm.
Gilbert de Botton Collection,
Switzerland.

88
Sleeping Figure. 1974.
Oil on canvas,
78 × 58 in. / 198 × 147.5 cm.
A. Carter Pottash Collection.

89
Three Portraits. Posthumous Portrait of George Dyer,
Self-Portrait, Portrait of Lucian Freud. 1973.
Triptych.
Oil on canvas,
each panel 78 × 58 in. / 198 × 147.5 cm.
Private collection.

90
Triptych. March. 1974.
Oil on canvas,
each panel 78 × 58 in. / 198 × 147.5 cm.
Private collection, Madrid.

91
Self-Portrait. 1973.
Oil on canvas,
78 × 58 in. / 198 × 147.5 cm.
Private collection.

92
Study for a Human Body (Man Turning on the Light). 1973-74.
Oil and acrylic on canvas,
78 × 58 in. / 198 × 147.5 cm.
The Royal College of Art, London.

93
Three Studies for Self-Portrait. 1974.
Small triptych.
Oil on canvas,
each panel 14 × 12 in. / 35.5 × 30.5 cm.
Carlos Haime Collection, Bogotá.

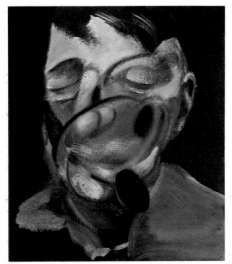

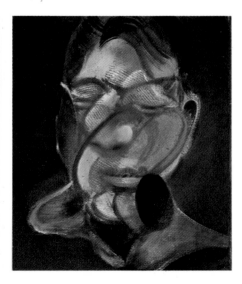

94
Three Figures and Portrait. 1975.
Oil and pastel on canvas,
78 × 58 in. / 198 × 147.5 cm.
The Tate Gallery, London.

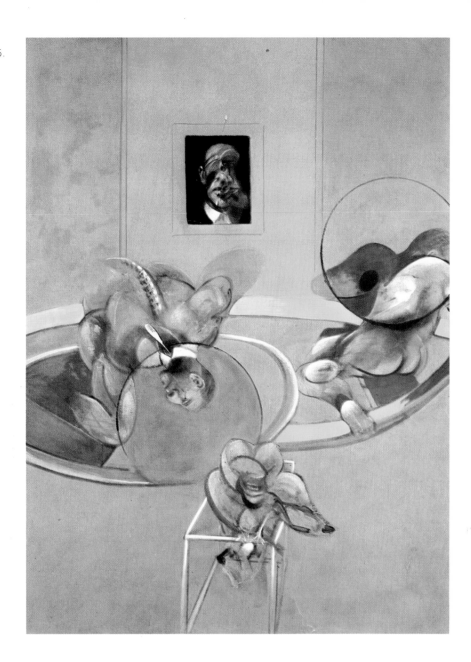

95
Three Studies for Self-Portrait. 1976.
Small triptych.
Oil on canvas,
each panel 14 × 12 in. / 35.5 × 30.5 cm.
Private Collection, Geneva.

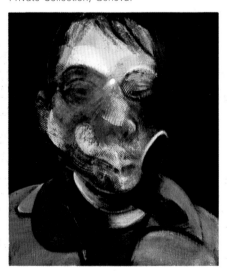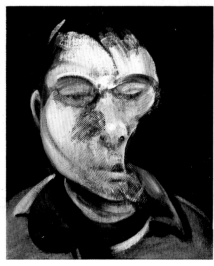

96
Three Studies for a Portrait (Peter Beard). 1975.
Small triptych.
Oil on canvas,
each panel 14 × 12 in. / 35.5 × 30.5 cm.
Private collection, Paris.

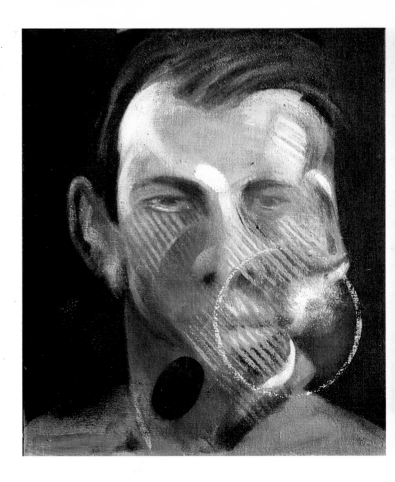

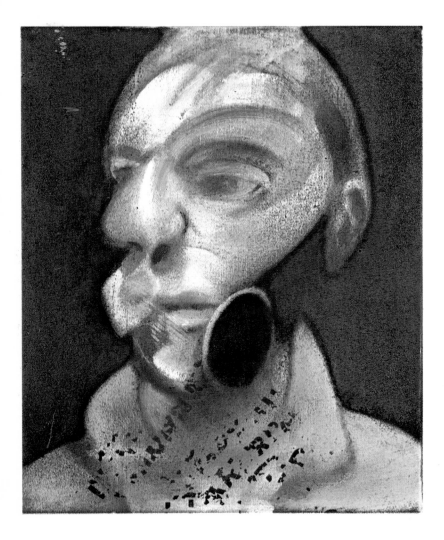

97
Self-Portrait. 1975.
Oil on canvas,
14 × 12 in. / 35.5 × 30.5 cm.
Private collection.

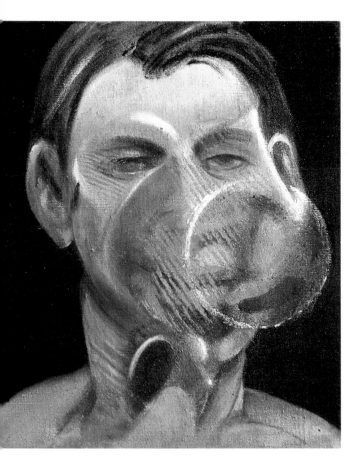
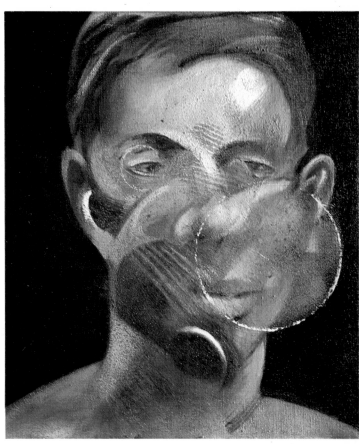

98
Three Studies for a Portrait of Peter Beard. 1975.
Small triptych.
Oil on canvas,
each panel 14 × 12 in. / 35.5 × 30.5 cm.
Private collection.

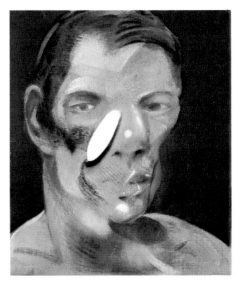
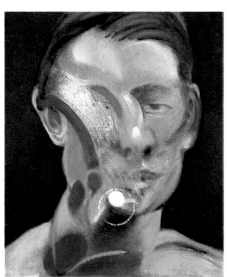
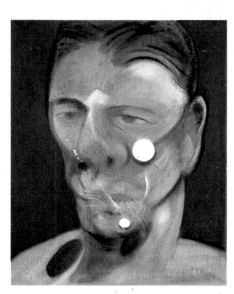

99
Portrait of a Dwarf. 1975.
Oil on canvas,
62 ½ × 23 in. / 158.5 × 58.5 cm.
Private collection, Sydney, Australia.

Right

100
Figure Writing Reflected in a Mirror. 1976.
Oil on canvas,
78 × 58 in. / 198 × 147.5 cm.
Private collection.

101
Studies from the Human Body. 1975.
Oil on canvas,
78 × 58 in. / 198 × 147.5 cm.
Gilbert de Botton Collection, Switzerland.

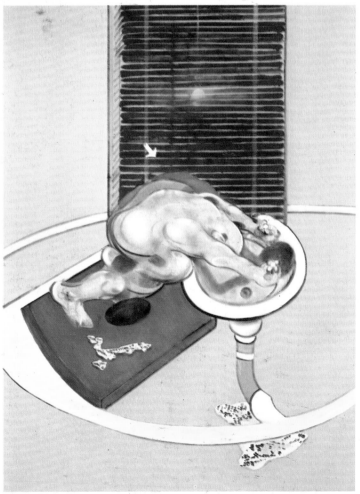

102
Figure at a Washbasin. 1976.
Oil on canvas,
78 × 58 in. / 198 × 147.5 cm.
Museo de Arte Contemporáneo, Caracas.

Figure in Movement. 1976.
Oil on canvas,
78 × 58 in. / 198 × 147.5 cm.
Private collection.

104
Triptych. 1976.
Oil and pastel on canvas,
each panel 78 × 58 in. / 198 × 147.5 cm.
Private collection, France.

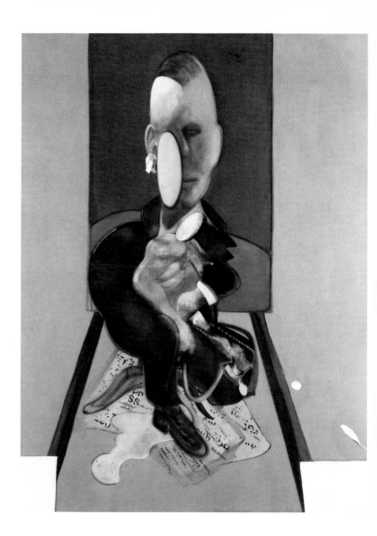

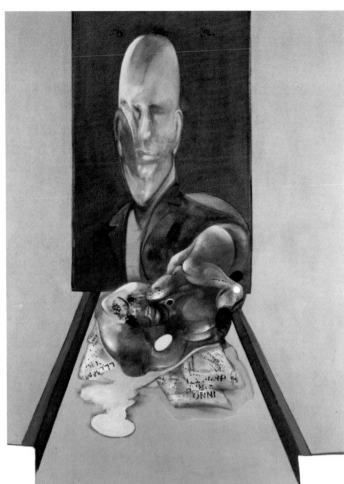

105
Triptych. 1974-77.
Oil and pastel on canvas,
each panel 78 × 58 in. / 198 × 147.5 cm.
Marlborough International Fine Art.

106
Study for Portrait. 1977.
Oil on canvas,
78 × 58 in. / 198 × 147.5 cm.
Private collection.

107
Portrait of Michel Leiris. 1976.
Oil on canvas,
14 × 12 in. / 35.5 × 30.5 cm.
Louise and Michel Leiris Collection, Paris.

108
Study for Portrait (Michel Leiris). 1978.
Oil on canvas,
14 × 12 in. / 35.5 × 30.5 cm.
Louise and Michel Leiris Collection, Paris.

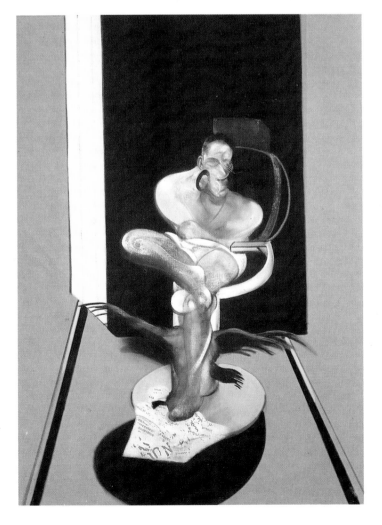

109
Seated Figure. 1977.
Oil on canvas,
78 × 58 in. / 198 × 147.5 cm.
Mrs Susan Lloyd Collection, Nassau.

110
Two Studies for Self-Portrait. 1977.
Diptych.
Oil on canvas,
each panel 14 × 12 in. / 35.5 × 30.5 cm.
Private collection.

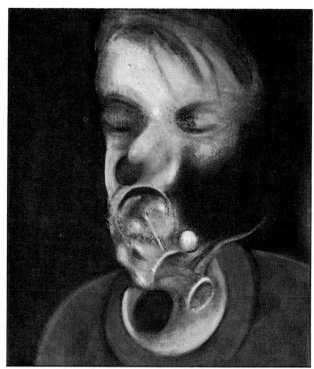

111
Two Studies for Portrait of Richard Chopping. 1978.
Diptych.
Oil on canvas,
each panel 14 × 12 in. / 35.5 × 30.5 cm.
Private collection.

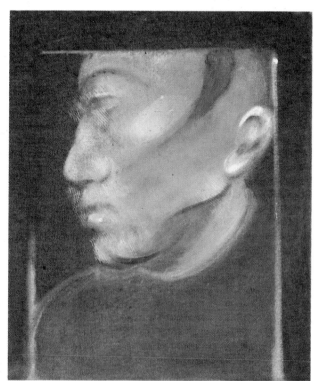

112
Landscape. 1978.
Oil and pastel on canvas,
78 × 58 in. / 198 × 147.5 cm.
Private collection.

113
Self-Portrait. 1978.
Oil on canvas,
78 × 58 in. / 198 × 147.5 cm.
Private collection.

114
Study for Portrait. 1978.
Oil on canvas,
78 × 58 in. / 198 × 147.5 cm.
Private collection.

115
Seated Figure. 1978.
Oil on canvas,
78 × 58 in. / 198 × 147.5 cm.
Private collection.

116
Figure in Movement. 1978.
Oil and pastel on canvas,
78 × 58 in. / 198 × 147.5 cm.
Private collection, Los Angeles.

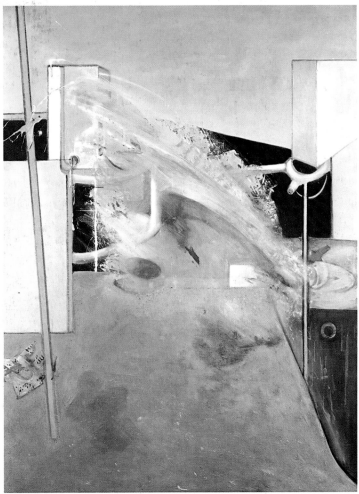

117
Jet of Water. 1979.
Oil on canvas,
78 × 58 in. / 198 × 147.5 cm.
Private collection, Switzerland.

118
Painting. 1978.
Oil on canvas,
78 × 58 in. / 198 × 147.5 cm.
Private collection.

119
Triptych - Studies of the Human Body. 1979.
Oil on canvas,
each panel 78 × 58 in. / 198 × 147.5 cm.
Private collection.

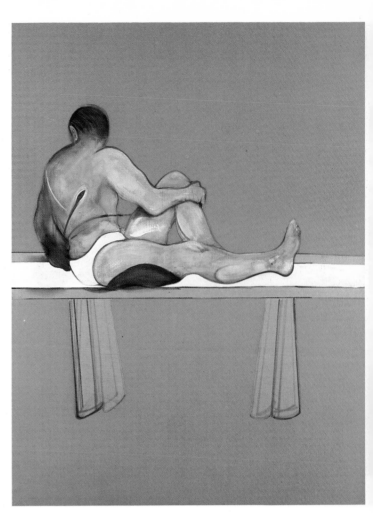

120
Seated Figure. 1979.
Oil on canvas,
78 × 58 in. / 198 × 147.5 cm.
Private collection, Japan.

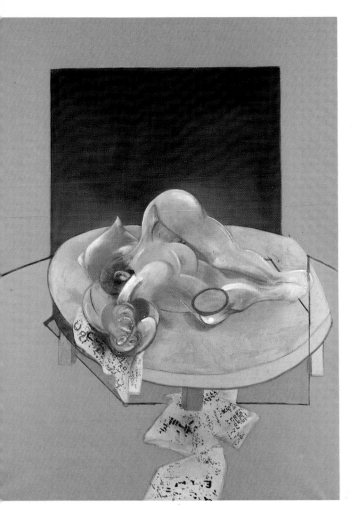

121
Three Studies for Self-Portrait. 1979.
Small triptych.
Oil on canvas,
each panel 14 ¾ × 12 ½ in. / 37.5 × 31.8 cm.
Private collection.

Two Seated Figures. 1979.
Oil on canvas,
78 × 58 in. / 198 × 147.5 cm.
Galerie Beyeler, Basle.

123
Sphinx - Portrait of Muriel Belcher. 1979.
Oil on canvas,
78 × 58 in. / 198 × 147.5 cm.
National Museum of Modern Art, Tokyo.

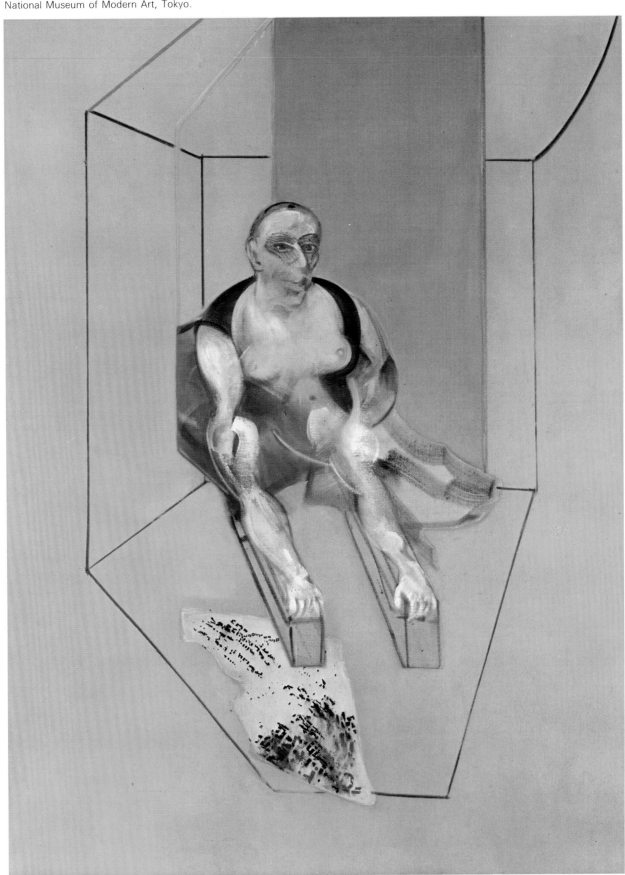

124
Three Studies for a Portrait of John Edwards. 1980.
Small triptych.
Oil on canvas,
each panel 14 × 12 in. / 35.5 × 30.5 cm.
Private collection, New York.

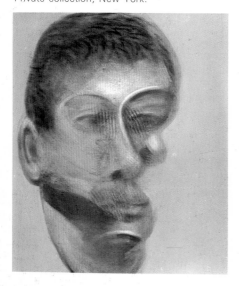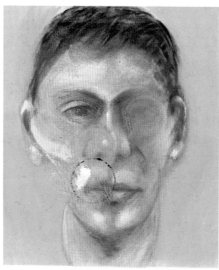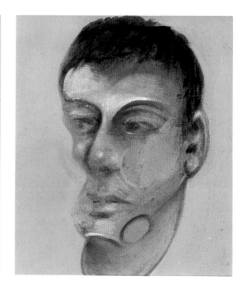

125
Study for Self-Portrait. 1980.
Oil on canvas,
14 × 12 in. / 35.5 × 30.5 cm.
Private collection.

Right

126
Carcase of Meat and Bird of Prey. 1980.
Oil and pastel on canvas,
78 × 58 in. / 198 × 147.5 cm.
Private collection, Paris.

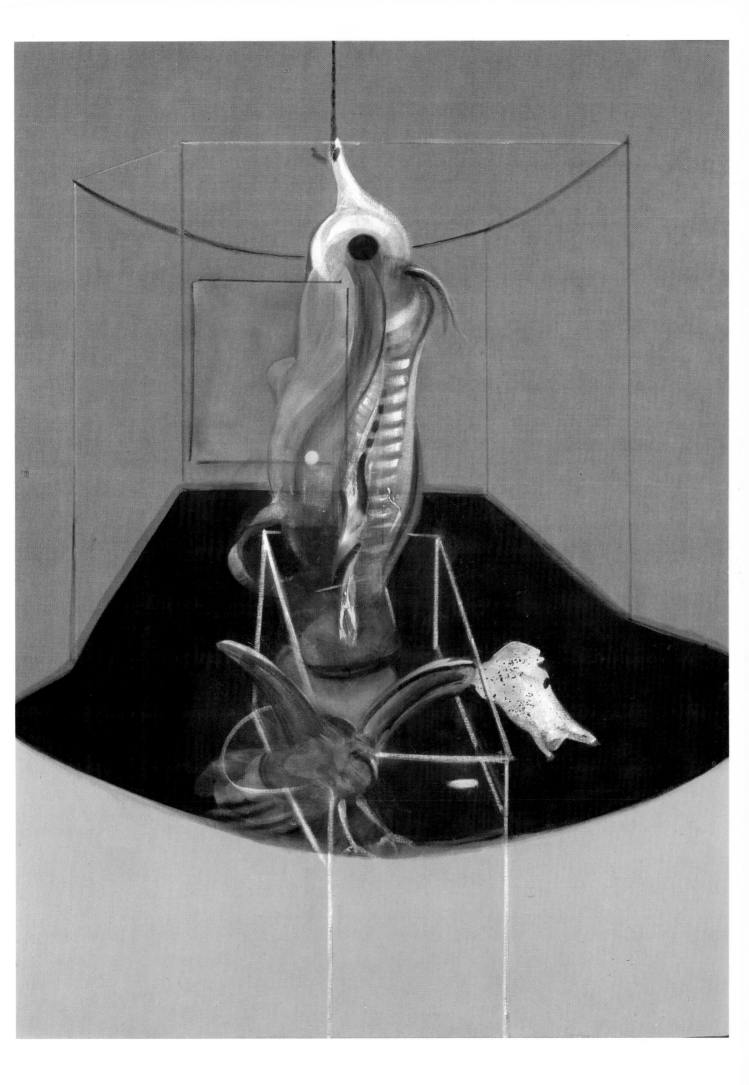

127
Study for Portrait with Bird in Flight. 1980.
Oil on canvas,
78 × 58 in. / 198 × 147.5 cm.
Private collection, Toronto.

128
Study of a Man Talking. 1981.
Oil on canvas,
78 × 58 in. / 198 × 147.5 cm.
Private collection, Berne.

129
Water from a Running Tap. 1982.
Oil on canvas,
78 × 58 in. / 198 × 147.5 cm.
Private collection.

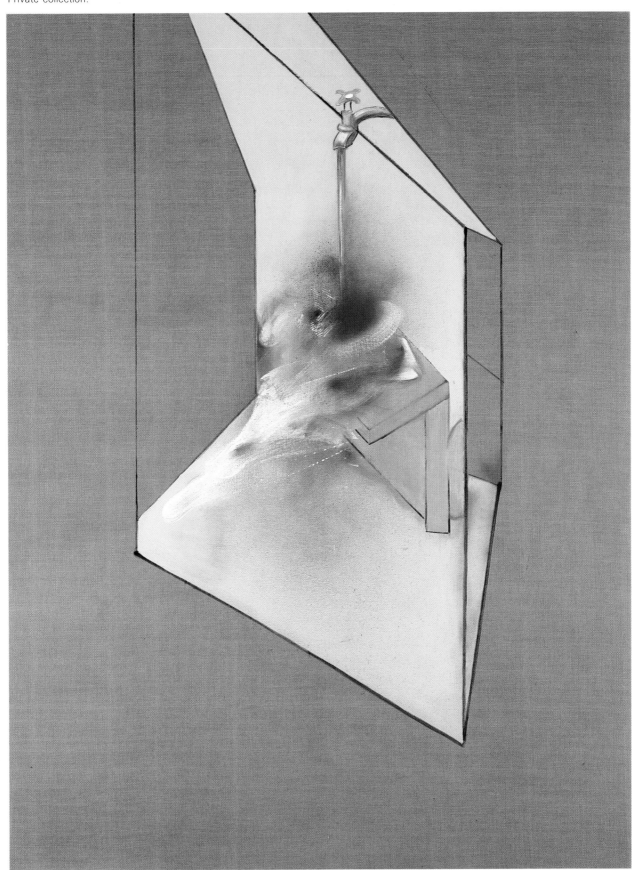

130
Triptych inspired by the Oresteia of Aeschylus. 1981.
Oil on canvas,
each panel 78 × 58 in. / 198 × 147.5 cm.
Private collection.

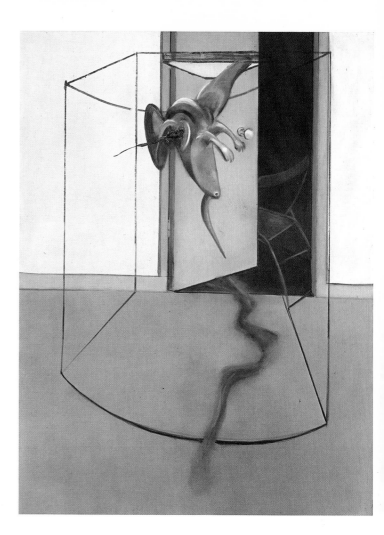

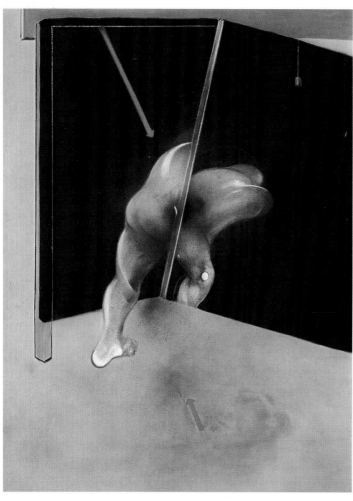

131
Study from the Human Body. 1981.
Oil on canvas,
78 × 58 in. / 198 × 147.5 cm.
Private collection, New York.

132
Study of the Human Body. 1982.
Oil and pastel on canvas,
78 × 58 in. / 198 × 147.5 cm.
Musée National d'Art Moderne,
Centre Georges Pompidou, Paris.

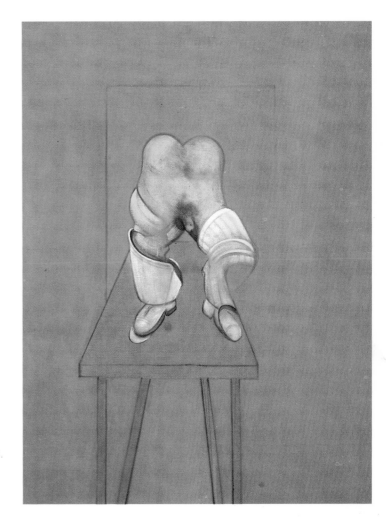

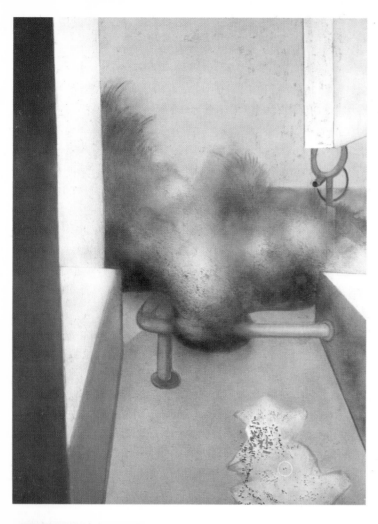

133
Sand Dune. 1981.
Oil and pastel on canvas,
78 × 58 in. / 198 × 147.5 cm.
Private collection.

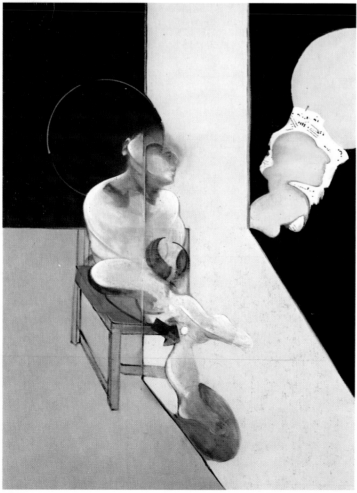

134
Study for Portrait. 1981.
Oil on canvas,
78 × 58 in. / 198 × 147.5 cm.
Private collection, Hartford, Connecticut.

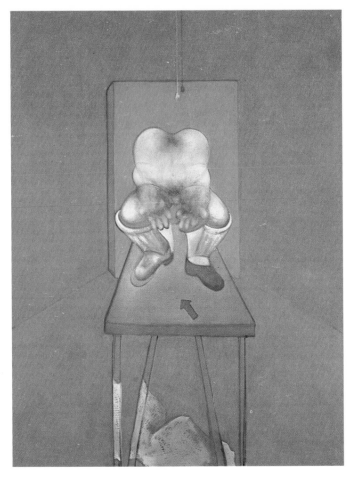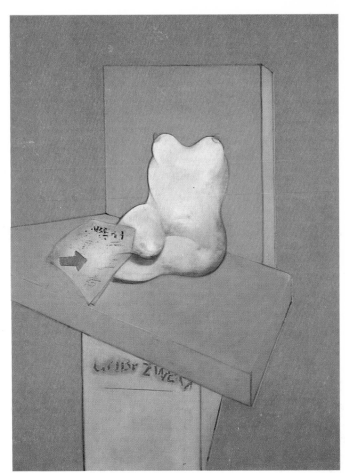

135
Diptych. 1982-84.
Study from the Human Body. 1982-84.
Study of the Human Body - from a Drawing by Ingres. 1982.
Oil and pastel on canvas,
each panel 78 × 58 in. / 198 × 147.5 cm.
Marlborough International Fine Art.

136
Three Studies for Portrait (Mick Jagger). 1982.
Small triptych.
Oil and pastel on canvas,
each panel 14 × 12 in. / 35.5 × 30.5 cm.
Paul Jacques Schupf Collection.

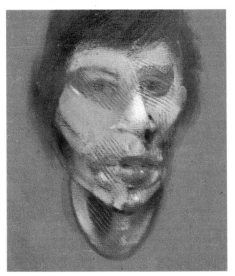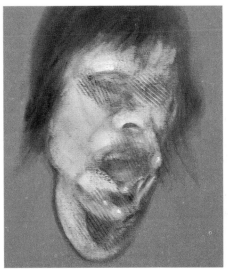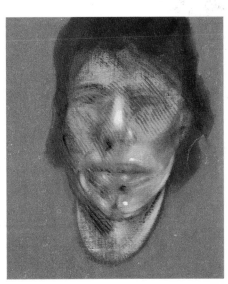

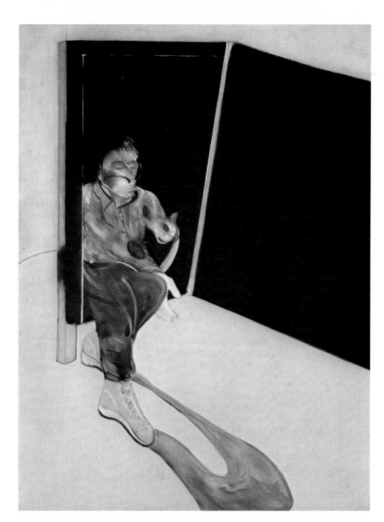

137
Study for Self-Portrait. 1981.
Oil on canvas,
78 × 58 in. / 198 × 147.5 cm.
Von der Heydt Museum,
Wuppertal.

138
Study for Self-Portrait. 1982.
Oil on canvas,
78 × 58 in. / 198 × 147.5 cm.
Private collection, New York.

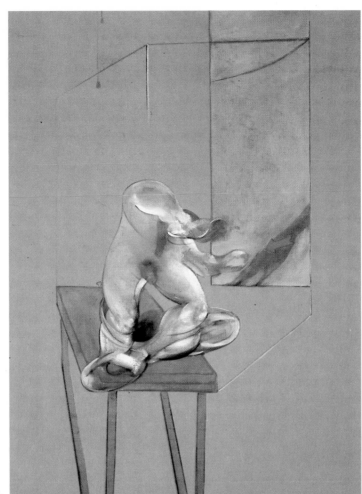

139
Study from the Human Body.
Figure in Movement. 1982.
Oil on canvas,
78 × 58 in. / 198 × 147.5 cm.
Marlborough International Fine Art.

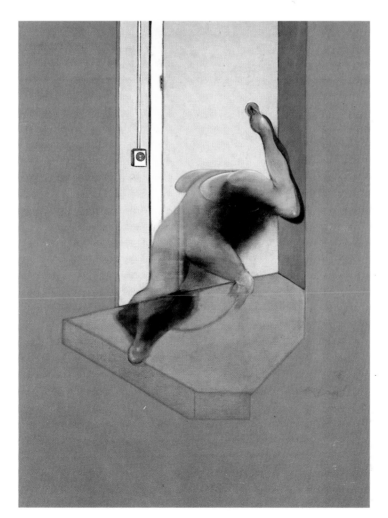

140
Study from the Human Body.
1983.
Oil and pastel on canvas,
78 × 58 in. / 198 × 147.5 cm.
Menil Foundation Collection,
Houston.

141
Triptych. 1983.
Oil and pastel on canvas,
each panel 78 × 58 in. / 198 × 147.5 cm.
Marlborough International Fine Art.

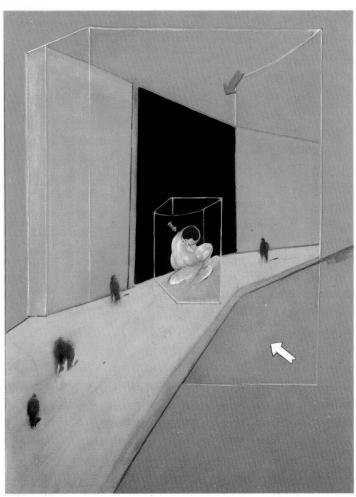

142
Statue and Figures in a Street. 1983.
Oil and pastel on canvas,
78 × 58 in. / 198 × 147.5 cm.
Private collection, New York.

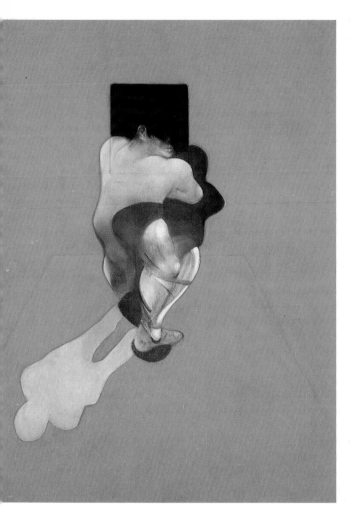

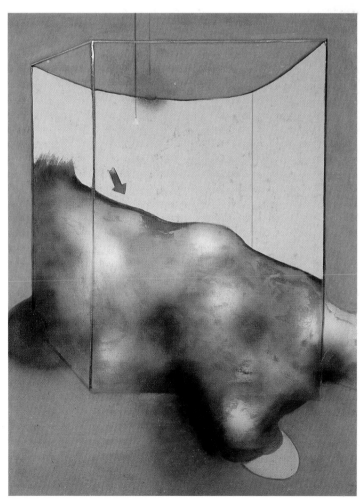

143
Sand Dune. 1983.
Oil and pastel on canvas,
78 × 58 in. / 198 × 147.5 cm.
Ernst Beyeler Collection, Basle.

144
Three Studies for a Portrait of John Edwards. 1984.
Triptych.
Oil on canvas,
each panel 78 × 58 in. / 198 × 147.5 cm.
Property of the Artist.

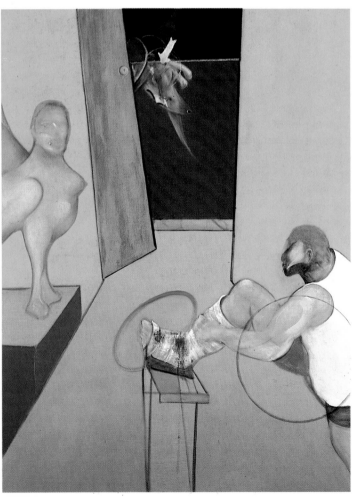

145
Œdipus and the Sphinx, after Ingres. 1983.
Oil on canvas,
78 × 58 in. / 198 × 147.5 cm.
Private collection.

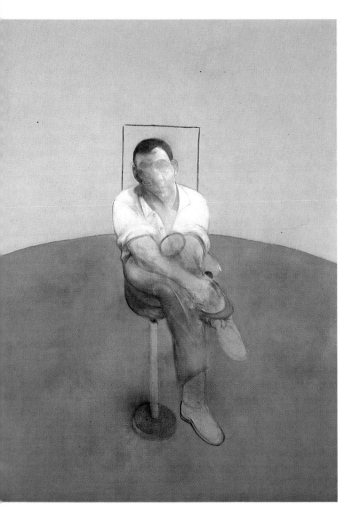

146
Study for a Portrait of John Edwards. 1985.
Oil on canvas,
78 × 58 in. / 198 × 147.5 cm.
Marlborough International Fine Art.

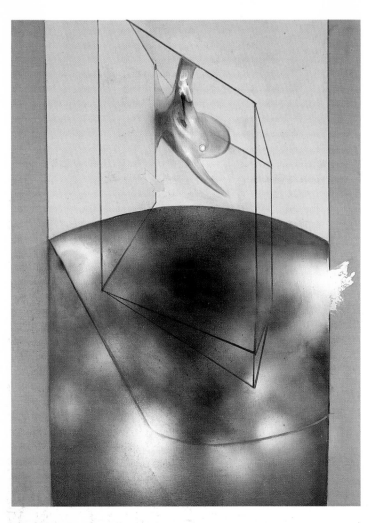

147
Painting. March 1985.
Oil on canvas,
78 × 58 in. / 198 × 147.5 cm.
Property of the Artist.

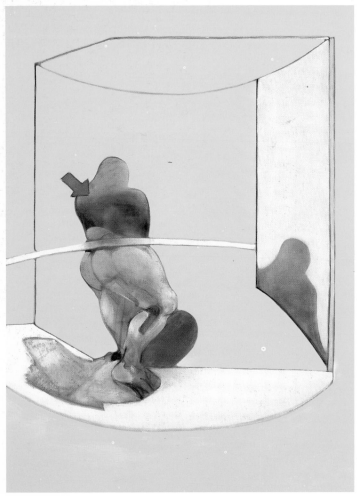

148
Study from the Human Body. 1986.
Oil and pastel on canvas,
78 × 58 in. / 198 × 147.5 cm.
Marlborough International Fine Art.

149
Figure in Movement. 1985.
Oil on canvas,
78 × 58 in. / 198 × 147.5 cm.
Private collection.

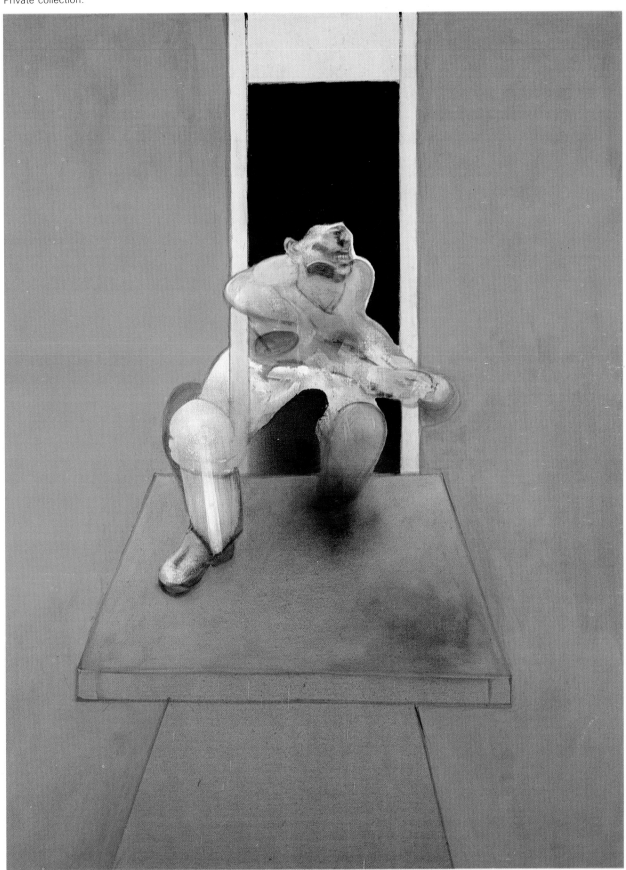

150
Study for Self-Portrait. 1985-86.
Triptych.
Oil on canvas,
each panel 78 × 58 in. / 198 × 147.5 cm.
Marlborough International Fine Art.

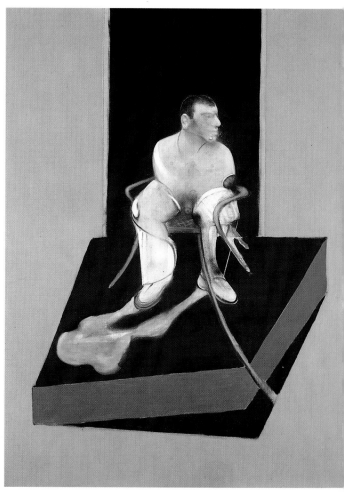

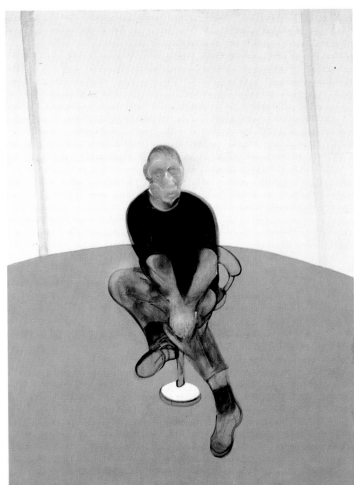

151
Triptych. 1986-87.
Oil and pastel on canvas,
each panel, 78 × 58 in. / 198 × 147.5 cm.
Property of the Artist.

152
Triptych. 1987.
Oil and pastel on canvas,
each panel 78 × 58 in. / 198 × 147.5 cm.
Property of the Artist.

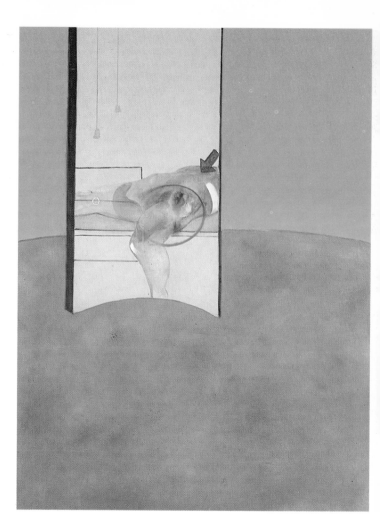

153
Blood on the Floor. 1986.
Oil and pastel on canvas,
78 × 58 in. / 198 × 147.5 cm.
Property of the Artist.

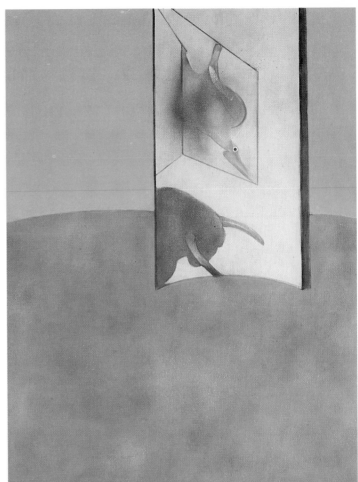

154
Study for Portrait of John Edwards. 1986.
Oil and pastel on canvas,
78 × 58 in. / 198 × 147.5 cm.
Marlborough International Fine Art.

155
Study from Human Body. 1987.
Oil and pastel on canvas,
77 ¾ × 58 in. / 197.5 × 147.5 cm.
Private collection.

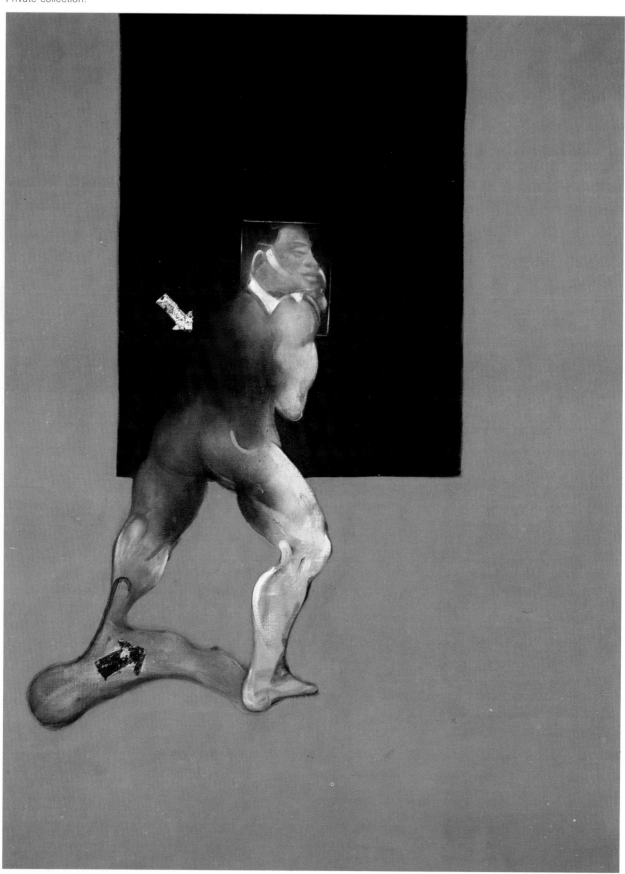

LIST OF WORKS

1
Three Studies for Figures at
the Base of a Crucifixion. 1944.
Oil and pastel on hardboard,
each panel 37 × 29 in. / 94 × 74 cm.
The Tate Gallery, London.

2
Figure in a Landscape. 1945.
Oil on canvas,
57 × 50 ½ in. / 145 × 128 cm.
The Tate Gallery, London.

3
Figure Study I. 1945-46.
Oil on canvas,
48 ½ × 41 ½ in. / 123 × 105.5 cm.
Private collection.

4
Painting. 1946.
Oil and tempera on canvas,
78 × 52 in. / 198 × 132 cm.
The Museum of Modern Art, New York.

5
Study from the Human Body. 1949.
Oil on canvas,
58 × 51 ½ in. / 147.5 × 131 cm.
The National Gallery of Victoria, Melbourne
(Felton Bequest).

6
Head I. 1948.
Oil and tempera on board,
40 ½ × 29 ½ in. / 103 × 75 cm.
Collection Richard S. Zeisler, New York.

7
Head VI. 1949.
Oil on canvas,
36 ¾ × 30 ¼ in. / 93 × 77 cm.
The Arts Council of Great Britain, London.

8
Head III. 1949.
Oil on canvas,
32 × 26 in. / 81 × 66 cm.
Private collection.

9
Study for Crouching Nude. 1952.
Oil on canvas,
78 × 54 in. / 198 × 137 cm.
The Detroit Institute of Arts
(Gift of Dr. Wilhelm R. Valentiner).

10
Three Studies of the Human Head. 1953.
Triptych.
Oil on canvas,
each panel 24 × 20 in. / 61 × 51 cm.
Private collection.

11
Study for a Portrait. 1953.
Oil on canvas,
60 × 46 ½ in. / 152.5 × 118 cm.
Kunsthalle, Hamburg.

12
Study after Velázquez's Portrait of
Pope Innocent X. 1953.
Oil on canvas,
60 ¼ × 46 ½ in. / 153 × 118 cm.
Des Moines Art Center,
Coffin Fine Arts Trust Fund, 1980.

13
Dog. 1952.
Oil on canvas,
78 ¼ × 54 ¼ in. / 199 × 138 cm.
The Museum of Modern Art, New York.

14
Chimpanzee. 1955.
Oil on canvas,
60 × 46 in. / 152.5 × 117 cm.
Staatsgalerie, Stuttgart.

15
Man with Dog. 1953.
Oil on canvas,
59 ⅞ × 46 in. / 152 × 117 cm.
Albright-Knox Art Gallery, Buffalo, New York
(Gift of Seymour H. Knox, 1955).

16
Two Figures. 1953.
Oil on canvas,
60 × 45 ⅞ in. / 152.5 × 116.5 cm.
Private collection.

17
Study for Portrait of Van Gogh II. 1957.
Oil on canvas,
78 × 56 in. / 198 × 142 cm.
Collection Edwin Janss, Thousand Oaks,
California.

18
Study for Portrait of Van Gogh VI. 1957.
Oil on canvas,
79 ¾ × 56 in. / 202.5 × 142 cm.
The Arts Council of Great Britain, London.

19
Study for Three Heads. 1962.
Small triptych.
Oil on canvas,
each panel 14 × 12 in. / 35.5 × 30.5 cm.
Collection William S. Paley, New York.

20
Study from Innocent X. 1962.
Oil on canvas,
78 × 57 ⅛ in. / 198 × 145 cm.
Collection M. Riklis.

21
Three Studies for a Crucifixion. 1962.
Triptych.
Oil on canvas,
each panel 78 × 57 in. / 198 × 145 cm.
The Solomon R. Guggenheim Museum,
New York.

22
Lying Figure with Hypodermic Syringe. 1963.
Oil on canvas,
78 × 57 in. / 198 × 145 cm.
Private collection, Switzerland.

23
Three Studies for Portrait of George Dyer
(on light ground). 1964.
Small triptych.
Oil on canvas,
each panel 14 × 12 in. / 35.5 × 30.5 cm.
Private collection.

24
Double Portrait of Lucian Freud and
Frank Auerbach. 1964.
Diptych.
Oil on canvas,
each panel 65 × 56 ⅜ in. / 165 × 145 cm.
Moderna Museet, Stockholm.

25
Three Studies for Head of Isabel
Rawsthorne. 1965.
Small triptych.
Oil on canvas,
each panel 14 × 12 in. / 35.5 × 30.5 cm.
Robert and Lisa Sainsbury Collection,
University of East Anglia, Norwich.

26
Study for Portrait (Isabel Rawsthorne). 1964.
Oil on canvas,
78 × 58 in. / 198 × 147.5 cm.
Private collection.

27
Three Figures in a Room. 1964.
Triptych.
Oil on canvas,
each panel 78 × 57 ⅞ in. / 198 × 147 cm.
Musée National d'Art Moderne,
Centre Georges Pompidou, Paris.

28
Three Studies for Portrait of Lucian Freud.
1965.
Small triptych.
Oil on canvas,
each panel 14 × 12 in. / 35.5 × 30.5 cm.
Private collection.

29
Portrait of Lucian Freud (on Orange
Couch). 1965.
Oil on canvas,
61 ½ × 54 ¾ in. / 156 × 139 cm.
Private collection.

30
Crucifixion. 1965.
Triptych.
Oil on canvas,
each panel 77 ⅝ × 57 ⅞ in. / 197.2 × 147 cm.
Staatsgalerie Moderner Kunst, Munich
(Gift of the Galerie-Vereins, Munich eV).

31
After Muybridge — Study of the Human
Figure in Motion — Woman Emptying a Bowl
of Water, and Paralytic Child on All Fours.
1965.
Oil on canvas,
78 × 58 in. / 198 × 147.5 cm.
Stedelijk Museum, Amsterdam.

32
Three Studies of Isabel Rawsthorne
(on White Ground). 1965.
Small triptych.
Oil on canvas,
each panel 14 × 12 in. / 35.5 × 30.5 cm.
Private collection.

33
Three Studies of Isabel Rawsthorne
(on Light Ground). 1965.
Small triptych.
Oil on canvas,
each panel 14 × 12 in. / 35.5 × 30.5 cm.
Private collection.

34
Three Studies of Isabel Rawsthorne. 1966.
Small triptych.
Oil on canvas,
each panel 14 × 12 in. / 35.5 × 30.5 cm.
Private collection, Paris.

35
Study of Isabel Rawsthorne. 1966.
Oil on canvas,
14 × 12 in. / 35.5 × 30.5 cm.
Louise and Michel Leiris Collection, Paris.

36
Portrait of George Dyer Crouching. 1966.
Oil on canvas,
78 × 58 in. / 198 × 147.5 cm.
Private collection, Caracas.

37
Portrait of George Dyer Staring at Blind
Cord. 1966.
Oil on canvas,
78 × 58 in. / 198 × 147.5 cm.
Private collection.

38
Portrait of George Dyer Talking. 1966.
Oil on canvas,
78 × 58 in. / 198 × 147.5 cm.
Private collection, New York.

39
Three Studies for Portrait of Lucian Freud.
1966.
Triptych.
Oil on canvas,
each panel 78 × 58 in. / 198 × 147.5 cm.
Marlborough International Fine Art.

40
Lying Figure. 1966.
Oil on canvas,
78 × 58 in. / 198 × 147.5 cm.
Museo Español de Arte Contemporáneo,
Madrid.

41
Three Studies of Muriel Belcher. 1966.
Small triptych.
Oil on canvas,
each panel 14 × 12 in. / 35.5 × 30.5 cm.
Private collection.

42
Three Studies of George Dyer. 1966.
Small triptych.
Oil on canvas,
each panel 14 × 12 in. / 35.5 × 30.5 cm.
Private collection, New York.

43
Study for Head of George Dyer. 1967.
Oil on canvas,
14 × 12 in. / 35.5 × 30.5 cm.
Private collection.

44
Portrait of George Dyer
Riding a Bicycle. 1966.
Oil on canvas,
78 × 58 in. / 198 × 147.5 cm.
Galerie Beyeler, Basle.

45
Study for Head of George Dyer and Isabel
Rawsthorne. 1967.
Diptych.
Oil on canvas,
each panel 14 × 12 in. / 35.5 × 30.5 cm.
Private collection, Italy.

46
Three Studies of Isabel Rawsthorne. 1967.
Oil on canvas,
46⅞ × 60 in. / 119 × 152.5 cm.
Staatliche Museen Preussischer Kulturbesitz,
Nationalgalerie, Berlin.

47
Portrait of Isabel Rawsthorne. 1966.
Oil on canvas,
26¾ × 18⅛ in. / 67 × 46 cm.
The Tate Gallery, London.

48
Triptych Inspired by T.S. Eliot's Poem
''Sweeney Agonistes''. 1967.
Oil on canvas,
each panel 78 × 58 in. / 198 × 147.5 cm.
Hirshhorn Museum and Sculpture Garden,
Smithsonian Institution, Washington, D.C.

49
Portrait of Isabel Rawsthorne Standing in a
Street in Soho. 1967.
Oil on canvas,
78 × 58 in. / 198 × 147.5 cm.
Staatliche Museen Preussischer Kulturbesitz,
Nationalgalerie, Berlin.

50
Three Studies of Isabel Rawsthorne. 1968.
Small triptych.
Oil on canvas,
each panel 14 × 12 in. / 35.5 × 30.5 cm.
Mrs Susan Lloyd Collection, Nassau.

51
Portrait of George Dyer in a Mirror. 1968.
Oil on canvas,
78 × 58 in. / 198 × 147.5 cm.
Thyssen-Bornemisza Collection, Lugano,
Switzerland.

52
Lying Figure. 1969.
Oil on canvas,
78 × 58 in. / 198 × 147.5 cm.
Galerie Beyeler, Basle.

53
Three Studies for Portrait. 1968.
Small triptych.
Oil on canvas,
each panel 14 × 12 in. / 35.5 × 30.5 cm.
Private collection.

54
Two Studies of George Dyer with Dog. 1968.
Oil on canvas,
78 × 58 in. / 198 × 147.5 cm.
Private collection.

55
Two Studies for a Portrait of George
Dyer. 1968.
Oil on canvas,
78 × 58 in. / 198 × 147.5 cm.
Sara Hildén Foundation,
Sara Hildén Art Museum, Tampere, Finland.

56
Two Figures Lying on a Bed with
Attendants. 1968.
Triptych.
Oil on canvas,
each panel 78 × 58 in. / 198 × 147.5 cm.
Present whereabouts unknown.

57
Three Studies of Lucian Freud. 1969.
Triptych.
Oil on canvas,
each panel 78 × 58 in. / 198 × 147.5 cm.
Private collection, Rome.

58
Three Studies of Henrietta Moraes. 1969.
Small triptych.
Oil on canvas,
each panel 14 × 12 in. / 35.5 × 30.5 cm.
Capricorn Art International, S. A. Collection,
Panama.

59
Three Studies of Henrietta Moraes. 1969.
Small triptych.
Oil on canvas,
each panel 14 × 12 in. / 35.5 × 30.5 cm.
Gilbert de Botton Collection, Switzerland.

60
Study of Henrietta Moraes Laughing 1969.
Oil on canvas,
14 × 12 in. / 35.5 × 30.5 cm.
Private collection.

61
Studies of George Dyer and Isabel
Rawsthorne. 1970.
Diptych.
Oil on canvas,
each panel 14 × 12 in. / 35.5 × 30.5 cm.
Private collection.

62
Three Studies of George Dyer. 1969.
Small triptych.
Oil on canvas,
each panel 14 × 12 in. / 35.5 × 30.5 cm.
Louisiana Museum, Humleback.

63
Self-Portrait. 1969.
Oil on canvas,
14 × 12 in. / 35.5 × 30.5 cm.
Private collection, London.

64
Study for Bullfight No. 1. 1969.
Oil on canvas,
78 × 58 in. / 198 × 147.5 cm.
Private collection.

65
Second Version of ''Study for Bullfight
No. 1''. 1969.
Oil on canvas,
78 × 58 in. / 198 × 147.5 cm.
Galerie Beyeler, Basle.

66
Three Studies of the Male Back. 1970.
Triptych.
Oil on canvas,
each panel 78 × 58 in. / 198 × 147.5 cm.
Kunsthaus, Zürich. Vereinigung Zürcher
Kunstfreunde.

67
Studies of the Human Body. 1970.
Triptych.
Oil on canvas,
each panel 78 × 58 in. / 198 × 147.5 cm.
Marlborough International Fine Art.

68
Studies of the Human Body. 1970.
Triptych.
Oil on canvas,
each panel 78 × 58 in. / 198 × 147.5 cm.
Jacques Hachuel Collection.

69
Self-Portrait. 1970.
Oil on canvas,
59⅞ × 58 in. / 152 × 147.5 cm.
Private collection.

70
Study for Portrait. 1970.
Oil on canvas,
78 × 58 in. / 198 × 147.5 cm.
Private collection, France.

71
Study for Portrait. 1971.
Oil on canvas,
78 × 58 in. / 198 × 147.5 cm.
Private collection, London.

72
Second version of ''Painting 1946''. 1971.
Oil on canvas,
78 × 58 in. / 198 × 147.5 cm.
Ludwig Museum, Cologne.

73
Triptych. 1971.
Oil on canvas,
each panel 78 × 58 in. / 198 × 147.5 cm.
Galerie Beyeler, Basle.

74
Female Nude Standing in a Doorway. 1972.
Oil on canvas,
78 × 58 in. / 198 × 147.5 cm.
Private collection, France.

75
Study for Portrait of Lucian Freud
(Sideways).
August, 1971.
Oil on canvas,
78 × 58 in. / 198 × 147.5 cm.
Private collection, London.